ACTIVE Business Travel

CHINA

创 易 商 务 旅 行 手 册

active 英中

anglo chinese communications

创
易

active 英中
anglo chinese communications
创易

Produced and published by Active UK China Publications
11 Gladbeck Way, EN2 7EL
London, UK
guide@activeukchina.com
www.activeukchina.com

Managing Editor: Yintong Betser
Sub Editor: Amanda McDonald, Brenda Williams,
                        Chris Buxton
Contents Contributors:
                        Yintong Betser, Han Li,
                        Richard Hirst, Ann Hirst,
                        Meng (Amy) Lei
Design: Hou Jing, Zhou Mojing

This handbook has been designed to be a guide to doing business in mainland China only. Hong Kong, Macau and Taiwan have different types of
business culture and etiquette. Although some similarities apply, it is not
recommended to use the guide for this purpose.

The information contained in this handbook has been compiled in good
faith. However, the contents may be subject to change, and the writers and
editorial team at Active UK China Publications cannot be held responsible
for any issues that may arise due to any inaccuracies contained herein.
Readers of the guide are encouraged to supplement the information contained within, with their own research.

ISBN 978-0-9556474-1-3

Active Business Travel – China
Contents

active
anglo chinese communications

英
中
创
易

Chapter 1

China Overview

Geography

China is the world's most populous country, and the third largest country by area, after Russia and Canada. China lies in Eastern Asia, bordered to the North by Mongolia and Russia; to the West by Kazakhstan, Kyrgyzstan, Tajikistan, India and Nepal; and to the South by Bhutan, Myanmar, Laos and Vietnam. To the East, China is linked to North Korea, and is lapped by the coastal waters of the South China Sea, East China Sea, and the Yellow Sea.

Area: 9,596,960 km² (approximately the same as Europe)
Land: 9,326,410 km²
Water: 270,550 km²
Population: 1.3 billion

The Chinese Central Government has divided China into different regions, which consist of 23 Provinces, 5 Autonomous Regions, 4 Municipalities and the 2 Special Administrative Regions of Hong Kong and Macao. Of the Municipalities, Beijing is the country's capital city situated in the North Eastern province of Hebei. The other Municipality cities are Tianjin,

Shanghai and Chongqing, which is now China's most populous city, as well as being one of the country's oldest settlements.

In addition, China has another 666 cities (11 of which have a population of over two million people, and 23 with populations of between one and two million people).

The two major rivers are Changjiang (the Yangtze River) and Huanghe (the Yellow River). Most of China's arable lands lie along these rivers; historically these rivers were central to China's major ancient civilisations.

At 6,380 km, the Yangtze River (Chang Jiang, literally translated as "Long River") is the longest river in China and the third longest in the world after the Amazon in South America and the Nile in Africa. The Yangtze River is seen as the physical dividing line between the North and South of China as it cuts its way from its source in the mountains on the borders of Tibet flowing in an easterly direction towards the East China Sea via an extensive delta.

The most impressive section of the river is made up of three Yangtze River gorges: the Qutang Gorge, Wuxia Gorge and Xiling Gorge, collectively

known as the Sanxia, or Three Gorges. Evidence of human activity was found in this area as far back as seven thousand years ago. The $25 billion Three Gorges Dam construction project on the Yangtze River was completed in 2006 and it is the largest hydro-electric dam in the world, measuring more than five times the size of the Hoover Dam!!

The Yangtze is flanked by industrial development zones reliant on the major transportation arteries, facilitating transportation to the inland provinces.

The Yellow River (or Huanghe River) is known as the mother river by the people, and at a distance of 5,464 kilometres, it is the second longest river in China after the Yangtze River. It is regarded by most Chinese people as being their spiritual home, acknowledged as the birthplace of ancient Chinese culture and the cradle of Chinese civilisation, as well as the most prosperous region in early Chinese history.

Climate

China lies mainly in the Northern temperate zone. From September/October to March/April the winds blow down from Siberia and the Mongolian Plateau, creating dry, cold winters and a temperature difference of up to 40°C between the North and South of the country.

Monsoon winds blow into China from the Eastern-facing seaboard in summer, bringing warm wet conditions to the coastal areas, with relatively little rainfall to the inland regions. Heavy rainfall regularly brings flooding to the major river valleys especially the areas surrounding the Yellow and Yangtze Rivers.

Average Temperatures

		J	F	M	A	M	J	J	A	S	O	N	D
Beijing	°F	25	28	39	55	68	77	79	77	68	55	39	27
	°C	-4	-2	4	13	20	25	26	25	20	13	4	-3
	Rain (mm)	4	5	8	18	33	78	224	170	58	18	9	3
Shanghai	°F	37	39	46	57	66	75	82	82	75	64	55	43
	°C	3	4	8	14	19	24	28	28	24	18	13	6
	Rain (mm)	47	61	84	95	104	174	145	137	138	69	52	37
Xi'an	°F	27	36	46	57	68	79	81	79	68	55	45	34
	°C	-3	2	8	14	20	26	27	26	20	13	7	1
	Rain (mm)	5	10	25	45	60	50	90	80	100	55	25	10
Guangzhou	°F	57	59	64	72	79	81	84	84	81	75	68	59
	°C	14	15	18	22	26	27	29	29	27	24	20	15
	Rain (mm)	35	65	95	185	265	270	245	230	170	65	45	20

Natural Resources

China has abundant mineral resources with over 160 kinds of minerals so far discovered. Total reserves rank third in the world. The minerals found include coal, iron ore, petroleum, natural gas, mercury, tin, tungsten, antimony, manganese, molybdenum, vanadium, magnetite, aluminium, lead, zinc and uranium. China's demand for iron ore is surging, due to the boom in the steel consumption corresponding with the nation's fast economic growth. China's natural reserves of rare earth metals have resulted in it becoming one of the world's leading exponents in the mining of such resources.

Population

China is the most populous country in the world, with over 20% of the world's population living within its borders. In January 2005, the

population in China reached 1.3 billion. The Chinese government introduced a 'one-child' policy per family, nearly thirty years ago to ensure that China, which has historically been prone to floods and famine, could feed all of its people. As a result, it is predicted that the population will continue to increase annually by about 10 million per year, hitting a peak of 1.46 billion in the 2030s. Despite the policy, the population has doubled over the past 50 years, and China's agriculture, energy supplies, urban infrastructure, education and housing have all come under increasing stress. Chronic air and water pollution problems are now evident in rural and urban areas throughout the country. All of these are issues that the Chinese government must resolve in order to improve the quality of life of the Chinese population.

About 62% of the population lives in the rural areas, however, as the country's urbanisation increases, millions of migrant workers are migrating from rural areas to earn their living in bigger towns and cities.

There are 56 official ethnic groups in China.

Han, the most predominant ethnic group, is accountable for over 93% of the population.

The other 55 are called 'ethnic minorities', whilst the remaining 7% is spread over half of the Chinese land area. The five provinces containing large minority populations are classified as 'autonomous regions'. These are Guangxi, Ningxia, Inner Mongolia, Tibet and Xinjiang.

History Outline

- 2200 – 1700 BC: Xia Dynasty
- 221 – 207 BC: 1st Emperor Qin Shihuang
- 206 BC – AD 220:   Han Dynasty
- 581 – 618:   Sui Dynasty
- 618 – 907:   Tang Dynasty
- 960 – 1279:   Song Dynasty
- 1206 – 1368:   Yuan Dynasty
- 1368 – 1644:   Ming Dynasty
- 1644 – 1911:   Qing Dynasty
- 1911 – 1949:   Transitional Period

Modern China

- October 1949:

  The Establishment of the People's Republic of China.

- 1956 - 1957:

  The Hundred Flowers Campaign. Greater intellectual freedom was encouraged, although the resulting criticism proved to be unacceptable to the government, hence many participants were put in jail or entitled with the derogatory term – 'Rightest'.

- 1958:

  The Great Leap Forward Campaign was an ambitious economic programme, aimed at utilising the vast population to rapidly transform China from an agrarian economy into a modern industrialised communist society.

- 1959 – 1961:

  Three years of natural disasters ensued. Poor economic policies combined with abnormal rainfall patterns caused widespread famine, resulting in many millions of deaths.

- 1966 – 1976:

  The Cultural Revolution. An almighty struggle for power within the Communist Party of China was fought out; enveloping large sections of

Chinese society and eventually bringing the entire country to its knees.

- 1978:

  Both the Reform and the Open Door policy were adopted in China, ending years of China's history of self seclusion.

- 1989:

  Tiananmen Square in Beijing was the venue for thousands of demonstrators including students, intellectuals and labour activists gathering together to voice complaints ranging from minor criticisms of Chinese rule through to calls for a fully-fledged democracy and the establishment of broader freedoms.

- 1992:

  A key year for the Chinese economy: Deng Xiaoping's well-known 'After Southern Tour Speech' called for bold, across-the-board economic reform in order to let market forces play a greater role in a "socialist economy with Chinese characteristics."

- 1997:
  Hong Kong was returned back to China from British rule.

- 1999:
  Macau was returned back to China from Portuguese rule.

- 2001:
  o China won its bid for the 2008 Olympics.
  o China was admitted to the World Trade Organisation in November 2001. Its entry ended a 15 year debate over whether China was entitled to full trading rights with capitalist countries.

- 2002:
  Vice President Hu Jintao became General Secretary of the Communist Party at the 16th Party Congress, succeeding President Jiang Zemin. Hu Jintao also assumed the Presidency in March 2003.

- 2003:
  Severe Acute Respiratory Syndrome (SARS), hit China in March 2003 to devastating effect within the gaze of the world's media.

- 2005:

  On 12th October, the second manned spacecraft Shenzhou VI ("Magic Vessel VI") carried two astronauts into space for a five-day mission in preparation for a manned space probe to the moon.

  On 21st July, The People's Bank of China announced that its currency will no longer be pegged to the US dollar and its exchange rate will float with reference to a basket of currencies.

The Chinese Communist Party and the Government

The political system in the People's Republic of China (PRC) takes place in a framework of a single-party socialist republic. State power within the PRC is exercised through the Communist Party, the Central Government and their provincial and local counterparts. Under

the dual leadership system, each local bureau or office is under the theoretically co-equal authority of the local leader and the leader of the corresponding office, bureau or ministry at the next level up.

Apart from the Communist Party, there are eight other democratic parties, although none of these parties generates significant influence. The Communist Party has three main functions:

- It is the only political party with influence throughout the country.
- The state carries out policies determined by the Party.
- The People's Liberation Army which is led by the Communist Party holds a special position in the government.

The primary organs of State power are the National People's Congress (NPC), the President and the State Council. The National People's Congress meets annually for about two weeks to review and approve major new policy directions, laws, the budget and major personnel changes.

The State Council (or cabinet), namely the Central

People's Government, is the highest executive body of State power, as well as the highest body of State administration. The State Council is composed of a Premier, Vice Premiers, State Councillors, Ministers in charge of ministries and commissions, the Auditor General and the Secretary General.

The Central Military Commission of the People's Republic of China is the highest State military organisation with the responsibility of commanding the entire armed forces in the country.

The Supreme People's Court is the highest trial organisation in the country and exercises its right of trial independently. It also holds the highest supervisory position over the trial practices of local people's courts and special people's courts at various levels. It reports its work to the National People's Congress and its Standing Committee.

The People's Procuratorates are State bodies for legal supervision. The Supreme People's Procuratorate is the highest procuratorial body and has to report its work to the NPC and its Standing Committee.

Laws in China

Chinese law is one of the oldest legal systems in the world and has traditionally been based on the direction of philosopher Confucius. Its primary facets are social control through moral education, coupled with a legal and criminal justice system based on a series of laws. There are also some elements of Soviet law within the system in operation in the People's Republic of China and some aspects of German law in the system initially operated in the Republic of China.

Religion

China is a country with a multitude of religious beliefs. The main religions are Buddhism, Confucianism, Taoism, Islam, Catholicism and Protestantism. Whilst each has a separate origin, Buddhism, Confucianism and Taoism have the most profound influence on China, its tradition and culture. They are intertwined and co-exist in the lives of the Chinese people.

Taoism (Daoism) is the only major religion that originates from Chinese roots and grew to maturity in Chinese soil - at the end of Eastern Han (25-220 AD) - and is based on ancient witchcraft and theories of immortality. Confucianism is more of a philosophy than a religion and its impact on business etiquette in China is fundamental (you can read more

about this in Chapter 5). Buddhism was founded in India but was introduced into the regions inhabited by the Han people during the 1st century AD. Islam arose in China's coastal cities in the Tang Dynasty (618 - 90 AD) and spread to many other areas with the return of the Mongolian army from its expeditions in the 13th century. Catholicism and Protestantism followed Buddhism and Islam but never established themselves as much as the Eastern religions.

Officially, the People's Republic of China encourages Atheism. However, Buddhist temples, Taoist temples and Muslim mosques can be easily found. Regular services for all religions including Catholic and Protestant, are available in all large cities.

Current Issues Facing China

The Chinese government is currently grappling

with the following key issues. That's why there are many favourable policies and regulations in place to help businesses - especially international organisations - to overcome them.

Population Issues

- Employment: The surplus of labour from the countryside and redundant workers from large state-owned factories has piled increasing pressure on the government.

- The poverty of the population: Unemployment and redundancy have led to poverty amongst a significant part of the population.
- Ageing: Since the end of 2000, China has become an ageing nation.

- Population Management: The State has diminished control over population distribution, labour market development, population censorship methods and the accuracy of the population statistics.

Environment Issues
- Water Pollution
- Air Pollution
- Noise Pollution
- Pollution by Solid Wastes
- Land Degradation
- Soil Erosion
- Endangered Forestry

Economic Growth Issues

The uneven distribution of social wealth has created major social and economic issues for the government and will influence the path of China's development in future. In addition, the growth of the number of people on low salaries is thwarting the government's efforts to stimulate domestic demand and reduce the economy's dependence on investment and trade.

active 英中
anglo chinese communications
创易

Chapter 2

Business Geography

–

Economic Strength
Distribution

The Chinese economy has historically been shaped by the country's key geographical location. More recently, sustained development has markedly increased the country's comprehensive economic strength. In the late 1970s, the Chinese government introduced economic reforms, bringing in elements of a free-market economy. The government also encouraged foreign investment, and together with the organic growth; it laid the groundwork for the modern Chinese market we see today.

Mainland China can be divided into three large economic regions, each with its own development characteristics, natural resources and conditions.

The Eastern Region consists of 12 provinces, autonomous regions and municipalities: Liaoning, Hebei, Beijing, Tianjin, Shandong, Jiangsu, Zhejiang, Shanghai, Fujian, Guangdong, Guangxi and Hainan.

The combined land mass of the Eastern Region is 129.37 km², which is 13.5% of the total land area of China. The Eastern Region faces the South China Sea and Pacific Ocean to the East, has a plain topography and is ideally suited to agriculture production. The Eastern Region is rich in natural resources such as aquatic products, oil, iron ore and salt. Due to its multi-faceted history, excellent geographical location, calibre of education, high cultural awareness of workers, level of technology and a strong industrial and agricultural foundation, the region holds a leading position in economic development. This is manifest in its stunning economic growth, massive modernisation programmes and the rising standard of living in the cities.

The Central Region consists of nine provinces, autonomous regions and municipalities: Heilongjiang, Jilin, Inner Mongolia, Shanxi, Henan, Hubei, Jiangxi, Anhui and Hunan.

The combined land mass of the Central Region is

281.75 km², which is 29.3% of the total area of land in China. The Central Region is surrounded to the North and South with higher grounds, whilst grain production is a key feature of the mainly flat central plains. The region is rich in energy sources and a variety of metal and non-metal mining products and is home to 80% of the country's coal reserves.

The Western Region consists of 11 provinces, autonomous regions and municipalities: Shaanxi, Gansu, Qinghai, Ningxia, Xinjiang, Sichuan, Chongqing, Yunnan, Guizhou and Tibet.

The combined land mass of the Western Region is 541.37 km² - 56.4% of the total area of China. The Western Region is fairly high in altitude and has a complex terrain with interspersed highlands, basins, deserts and grasslands. The majority of the region is cold and lacks water, therefore making it unsuitable for agricultural development. Due to its short exploitation history, there is a large economic development and technological management gap between the more developed Eastern and Northern regions and its Western counterparts. However, it has huge development potential due to its vast avail-ability of land and rich mining resources.

Seven Large Regions

The three economic regions reflect the differenc-es in the level of economic development in mod-ern day China. Due to its vast territory, China can be further sub-divided into seven large re-gions based on its regional economic framework and integrated economic advantage.

The Bohai Economic Region

Size: 112×104 km^2

Population: 260 million

The core cities of the region include Beijing, Tianjin, Shenyang, Dalian, Jinan, Qingdao, Shijiazhuang, Tangshan, Taiyuan, and Hohehot. The region is situated in the centre of North East China and is one of the most important areas in the country's policy guiding development.

Regional topography:

• The area is ideally situated, with strong political and economical potential. It contains the most advanced transportation network in the country, with a number of key motorway networks about to be developed. Compared to the rest of China, the area boasts high standards of education in science and technology and is ideally placed to deliver outstanding results in the field of advanced technological industry.

- Recent investment has resulted in the establishment of the three niche electronic industries in the region: micro-electronics, optics and computer manufacturing. In addition, biologically-engineered new materials and other types of Information Technology industries have seen major growth and development. The region also offers an abundance of rich natural resources of various mining products, including oil, iron ore, coal and sea, all playing an important role in China's reserves.
- Agriculture: the region has grain, cotton, fruit, aquatic products and growing bases in Hebei and Shandong.

North Eastern Economic Region

Size: 145×104 km^2

Population: 120 million

This region contains Heilongjiang, Jilin, Liaoning and Eastern Inner Mongolia.

Regional topography:

- The region has an advanced modern transportation network. Industrial strengths include petroleum chemical engineering, smelt metal mining machinery and steel production. The region also assumes a leading position in the country's transportation equipment manufacture infrastructure including automotive production. This, combined with the output generated from forestry make this region the country's largest base for heavy industry.

- The region's competitive advantages include access to rich resources and a good combination of different types of terrain. Oil, iron ore, coal, crops, sugar beet, log and livestock products each makes up a substantial proportion of the country's total resources. Water reserves are also copious in this Northern area of the country.
- The area is a key agricultural centre and an im-

portant base in the production of crops, logs, sugar beet and livestock.

The Yangtze Delta Economic Region

Size: 33×104 km²
Population: 168 million
This region includes Shanghai, the jurisdiction of Jiangsu, 14 cities in Zhejiang and 28 cities along the Yangtze River.

Regional topography:
- This region is the most economically prosperous and technologically advanced area of the country. And, there is still huge economic potential in the region that has yet to be fulfilled.
- In terms of human resource, there is a high level of skill amongst local people particularly in science and technology. With the general standard of education being higher here than in any other area of the country, the region is best equipped for further exploitation of the advanced technology industry.
- The region is geographically well situated and the sea, air and motorway transportation

network offers a competitive communication advantage. It forms the main communication thoroughfare between Central and Western China and the Asia-Pacific Economic Region, incorporating the Yangste River, and the South China Sea, with onward links throughout the world.

- The region is an important financial centre. Shanghai is home to the largest stock exchange centre in China as well as being one of the key financial centres in Asia. The city has further optimised its industrial structure, thus constantly consolidating the foundation for its economic growth. There are many Chinese and international banks in the area, providing fast and efficient financial services to organisations from all over the world. This is reflected in the skill base of the workforce, many of whom are highly qualified in the realms of finance, trade and business.

- An integrated economic region has been developed based on the light textiles industry and a combination of light and heavy industry. Automotive, steel and petroleum chemical engineering make up a third to a half of similar industries in the country overall.

- The area is home to many science, technology and engineering companies specialising in the following: photo-conductive fibres, lasers, biological engineering, marine engineering and micro-electronics. In addition, the region is also well utilised by manufacturers of automotives, electricity-generating equipment, metering instrumentation, ethane and processed products as well as ship builders.

Central Economic Region

Size: 87.12×104 km^2

Population: 313 million

This area includes Henan, Hubei, Hunan, Jiangxi and Anhui.

Regional topography:

- Located in the heart of China, the region acts as a buffer between the more economically developed Southern areas of the country and the less developed Eastern areas. The region also connects Shanghai, Yungang and Guangzhou, all three being seen to be key to the economic transformation of the country in terms of attracting foreign investment into China. The region is ideally situated as a communications hub with excellent regional and national transportation links.
- The region is strategically important in terms of both economic and science and technology development.
- The area is climatically advantageous for businesses in terms of its temperate climate, and suitable natural conditions for agricultural development.
- The region is of significant importance for paddy rice, cotton, fresh water products, rapeseed and other important primary products.
- The region is rich in coloured metals, water, en-

ergy, iron, non-metals and other resources.

- There is an emphasis on large volume water use in industry, forming an industrial belt along the river for metallurgy, textiles, automotive manufacture, chemical engineering and other industries.

South Eastern Coast Economic Region

Size: 29.93×104 km²

Population: 98 million

This area includes the Guangdong and Fujian provinces and Southern Zhejiang regions that border onto the South China Sea and Pacific Ocean.

Regional topography:

- The area borders onto the key economic territories of Hong Kong and Macau and the island of Taiwan, situated 100 miles off the mainland. Since the Chinese Reformation, the region has evolved economically to its current position as being ideally placed to develop foreign economic markets and innovative cutting-edge technological practices with many blue chip organisations represented in the region. In addition, the region offers a plethora of tourist-related activity, in particular Hong Kong is known across the world for its tourist attractions such as Disneyland and Ocean Park, as well as being the home to some of the world's finest hotels.

- The region is located in a sub-tropical area with temperate weather conditions, ideally suited for tropical crop production.

- The area has a rich reserve of Manganese coloured metals, rubber and a fairly rich water resource. Supplementing this, the area is highly engaged with electronics, chemically-engineered household products and top-grade consumables.

Unsurprisingly, with its very strong economic foundation, the South East Coast Economic Region is the most economically affluent of all of the seven regions listed.

South Western Economic Region

Size: 257×104 km²

Population: 250 million

This area includes the areas of Sichuan, Chongqing, Guizhou, Yunnan, Guangxi, Tibet, Hainan and Western areas of Guangdong (consisting of Zhanjiang, Maoming and Zhaoqing).

Regional topography:

- The area contains a diverse selection of natural resources including mining, water, and exploitable soil; and over half of China's total water and electricity output is generated within the region. The area is also rich with biological resources, with forestry becoming a key contributor to the economic stability of the area, as is the rapidly expanding tourism sector. However, poor infrastructure is impeding the level of resource development growth due to poor transportation and information networks and a comparatively low level of economy.

- With a combination of local resources, the main development in the region involves high energy input into the heavy chemical engineering industry including the production of steel, coloured metals and phosphor products, mechanics, light textiles and foodstuffs.

North Western Economic Region

Size: 419.89×104 km²

Population: 3.12 million

This area includes the areas of Shanxi, Gansu, Ningxia, Qinghai, Xinjiang and Inner Mongolia.

Regional topography:

- The North West Economic Region forms an important gateway to Central and Western Asia as well as Eastern Europe via the new Euro-Asia Continental Bridge, offering excellent communication links and enhancing the economic appeal of the region.

- The core industries that form the backbone of the region's infrastructure include coloured

metal smelting, petroleum chemical engineering, salt chemical engineering, mechanical production, energy production and material production.

- The region has a fairly poor climate and a fragile natural environment; however, resources are rich, especially of energy sources such as mining products and exploitable and usable soil.

- The overall economy of the region is fairly poor with only a few areas where economic activity flourishes. Many ethnic minorities are concentrated in this region and it acts as a key communications centre for the four largest ethnic minority municipalities consisting of the following: Xinjiang, Tibet, Ningxia and Inner Mongolia.

Chapter 3

Economic and Business Environment

AGRICULTURE

China is a vast country with nearly one fifth of the world population but only 7% of the world's cultivated land. Like other areas of the economy, agriculture has been liberalised from its previous restrictions and now has a more entrepreneurial footing. In 1978 Deng Xiaoping implemented the following reforms:

- The household responsibility system replaced the commune system. Farmers are now contracted to cultivate allotments and given the freedom to choose what is grown.
- The state monopoly for the purchase and marketing of agricultural products was ended.
- Many restrictive policies were abolished, allowing farmers to develop a diversified economy in rural areas and run township enterprises

Agriculture has also been experiencing rapid development, but by the end of 2005, 40% of China's population were living in cities. This figure is twice the number of 20 years ago and it is expected to continue rising. This shift in demography has placed new burdens on the government and on agriculture. To maintain the country's stability, farmers' wellbeing is at the top of the government's agenda. To narrow the income gap between rural and urban populations, the government took steps by abolishing the 2600 year old agricultural tax and increased subsidies to farmers by 14%.

INDUSTRY

Energy Resources Industry: China's energy supply and demand have both increased at an amazing pace. Its total energy consumption and energy generation grew by 14% and 13.5% respectively in 2006 alone. Thermal power accounts for the bulk of the energy generated, 83%, then 14% from hydro, 2% from nuclear and 0.1% from wind power.

Government policies point favourably towards alternative power sources. China's Renewable

Energy Law was introduced in January 2006. It decrees that 20% of total national energy consumption should come from renewable resources by 2020.

Coal resources – China has the world's third largest reserves of coal and is the largest producer. Coal mining is mainly to be found in the north of the country with around 70% of the country's total coal being transported to the energy hungry eastern coastal regions. The North China region has the largest coal output of the entire country, within which Shanxi is currently the largest coal-producing area.

Coal is still the chief means of meeting the energy demands of China's rapid industrial development, accounting for 74% of the total annual needs for electric power generation. Railways are still the predominant method of transportation for coal in China but severe underinvestment in the rail network means the system is operating at over-capacity, often giving rise to the late delivery of coal which leads to occasional power cuts and brownouts.

Meanwhile, environmental issues including pollution, health care and clean-up costs add more weight to the calls for the development of alternative energy sources.

The oil extraction industry - Whilst renewables are on the government's agenda, it is oil that is increasingly becoming the focus of China's geo-political strategy and remains one of the most important energy industries in China. From 1997 to 2005, China's annual crude oil output exceeded 160 million tons, ranking it fifth in the world.

Petroleum and natural gas are important energy resources. Several huge oil and gas projects are being developed to meet the country's energy demand. On going projects include Guangdong

LNG Terminal and Supply Project, the West to East Gas Project, coal liquefaction, natural gas exploration and the Bohai Bay exploration projects.

- Inland: Oil is extracted from the Changqing, Yumen and Kelamayi oil fields, oil and gas are also extracted from Talimu, Tulufan and Hami Basins, whilst natural gas is produced in Shanxi, Gansu and the Ningxia Basins.
- Further commercial quantities of oil and gas have been identified in areas such as the Bohai Sea, the North Yellow Sea, the mouth of the Pearl River, the Yingge Sea and Beibu Bay.

Electric Power Generation is the fastest growing sector of all industries. Power grid construction is at its fastest ever development with the main power grids now covering all urban conurbations and most rural areas.

Nuclear power has become the third most important method of electricity generation in China, after thermal and hydropower. China's nine completed nuclear power generating units now account for about 2.3% of the total power output. It is planned that a further 30 – 35 nuclear reactors will be built by 2020, which will then represent 4% of the country's total generating capacity.

Steel

China's massive steel industry produced over 10 million tons in 2006 and is by far the largest producer in the world. The biggest production areas are in the East and Northeast. In 2005, the government made steel industry consolidation a priority, focusing on creating large regional giants throughout the country. It is financially support-

ing the most promising steel enterprises such as Baosteel, Shougang in Beijing, Angang of Liaoning province and Wugang in Wuhan.

Automotive Industry

Machinery and transportation equipment have been the key products leading the boom in China's exports. The combined sectors have led the export table in the past 10 years. Their combined export value reached US$290.6bn in 2005.

As for the automotive industry itself, approximately 5.7m vehicles were produced in 2005, of which 3.9m were saloon cars. According to reports, total vehicle production capacity in China has reached 8 million units with another 2 million on the way. There were 6322 automotive enterprises in China at the end of 2006. China's major automotive companies are working hard to join the world market. China is now the 3rd largest auto producer and 2nd largest auto market in the world.

To further promote the use of clean car technologies and to reduce exhaust pollution, the government launched a R&D campaign for key "clean car" technologies. Now, test demonstrations of electric cars are underway in cities such as Beijing, Wuhan, Tianjin and Weihai. The International Fuel Cell Bus Demonstration Project that is supported by the United Nations is underway in Beijing and Shanghai.

Construction Industry

China's construction industry has experienced consistent growth over the last two decades. The infrastructure investment has focused heavily on roads, rail networks, bridges, ports and airports. With the 2008 Olympics taking place in Beijing and other northern cities, this has led to even more large projects being identified and a further increase in the number of international companies becoming involved with China. China expects to

build between 486 – 549 million m² of floor space annually in the first 20 years in the 21st century. The construction industry has contributed to the sustainable development of China's economy.

Transportation

According to the World Bank statistics, goods lost due to the poor transportation infrastructure during the 1990s accounted for up to 1% of China's GDP. At the same time, logistic costs account for 20% of the price for Chinese goods as opposed to only 10% for goods in the United States. Yet regardless of the deficiencies of China's transport infrastructure, China's economy has somehow still been able to thrust ahead. However, the government has recognised the situation and has substantially increased its investment in the expansion and modernisation of the transportation infrastructure.

Railways: By 2006, the railway network reached 77,000 km, which gives China the third largest railway network in the world. With 24,000 km of overhead electric powered railway lines, China has the second longest electrified railway network after Russia. It is predicted that by 2020, China's railways will extend to 120,000 km. Meanwhile, China is transporting 25% of the world's total freight volume over only 6% of the world's railway network.

- Since 1998, the speed of the Chinese railway has been successfully upgraded six times, across some 17,000km of track.

- The top speed of express trains increased from 120km to 160km per hour and passenger trains can reach a maximum speed of 200km per hour on some sections of trunk railways.

- The Qingzang Railway linking Geermu in Qinghai and Lhasa in Tibet is the highest railway in the world at an altitude of 4000m and half of its length is built on permafrost.
- The Maglev train connecting Pudong Airport with Shanghai city centre is currently the fastest train in the world.

Motorways ("expressways") – China has always treated motorways as one of the most important means of accelerating the development of its infrastructure. The investment in highway construction has increased enormously since 2000 owing to increased government attention. About 3,000km of motorway has been added per year to the existing network. By the beginning of 2006, the total length of motorways open to traffic reached 1.98 million km, making it the world's second largest road network. China's national highway skeleton system will be completed in 2008.

Ports and docks – China has 16 major shipping ports with a capacity of over 50 million tons per year. The ports in China bordering the sea are mainly used to transport coal, containers, imported iron ore and grain. Deep-water container docks have been built in Dalian, Tianjin, Qingdao, Shanghai, Ningbo, Xiamen and Shenzhen. The total throughput of some of the large ports has exceeded one hundred million tons. Shanghai, Shenzhen, Qingdao, Tianjin, Guangzhou, Xiamen, Ningbo and Dalian are now ranked amongst the world's best 50 container ports. Shanghai was the largest port in the world according to it's ranking in 2005.

By end of 2005, China's coastal ports had more than 2,500 medium size or larger berths. Their combined handling capacity was over 75 million standard containers a year, ranking China the world's largest for the 3rd successive year. By 2010, 35% of the world's shipping is expected to originate from China.

Civil Aviation
- The international carrier division of the Civil Aviation Administration of China (CAAC) was renamed Air China in 1988. It is the only airline to carry the national flag on its entire fleet.
- In 2002 the government merged the nine largest airlines into three regional groups based in

Beijing, Shanghai, and Guangzhou, respectively: Air China, China Eastern Airlines and China Southern Airlines. They operate the majority of China's external flights.

- By 2006, China had 138 civil airports with 1,567 routes.
- There are a total of 37 different airlines operating in China, handling approximately 160 million passengers, and 3 million tons of cargo.

SCIENCE AND TECHNOLOGY

China's Science and Technology industry has developed rapidly in line with the principles and strategic objectives set by the government. This is largely centred on research and development. China has built thousands of new high-tech development zones, a great many sci-tech research results have been put into use in production. By 2020, China's overall investment in research and development is forecasted to reach 2.5% of GDP, compared with 1.3% in 2005. The independent innovation capability, the comprehensive strength in learning basic science and frontier technology will smooth the way for China to become a truly innovative country in its own right.

China's Hi-Tech Industry

China's emerging technological expertise is built on a high concentration of skilled personnel and an open business environment. It also relies on the country's scientific, technological and economic strength as well as absorbing and taking advantage of international innovations, capital and management methods. Through the implementation of favourable policies and reforms of the hi-tech industry, productivity is on the increase.

Hi-Tech development is concentrated in the following areas:

- Electronics and information technology
- Bio-engineering and new medicine
- New materials and applications

- Advanced manufacturing technologies
- Aero and astronautics
- Marine engineering
- Nuclear applications
- New energy resources and high-efficiency energy-saving technologies
- Environmental protection
- Modern agriculture

Main Hubs for Software Production:
- Software Bases: Dongda, Qilu, Western, Changsha, Beijing, Tianjin Huayuan and Hubei.
- Software Parks: Hangzhou, Fuzhou, Jinlu, Xian, Dalian, Guangzhou, Shanghai, Nanjing, Changchun, Xiamen and Hefei.

Information Industry

The information industry is another mainstay of China's economy. It is ranked the 3rd largest in terms of added value which is at 1,130 billion yuan. The industry has outstripped other traditional industries on all fronts: output value, sales and profits.

Internet services and businesses include many aspects including internet education, internet banking, online business dealings, internet news, internet video services, charged mailing services and VOIP telephony, text messaging services, services for qualified personnel, online enquiry services, and internet games. All of these have continued to develop rapidly.

As for the telecommunications network, a basic transmission network with large capacity and of high speed is in place. It covers the whole country through optical cable which serves as the main technology for transmitting information, with satellite and digital microwave as supplementary systems.

China has also been involved in the construction of a number of international land and sea-bed optical cables - for instance, the construction of the 27,000 km Asia-Europe optical cable is the world's longest land system of its kind.

Industry facts:

- In 2006, the number of internet users had reached 137million, amongst which those using broadband had now exceeded 100million.
- In 2006, the number of people who use the internet via their mobile phones reached 17million.
- By the end of 2005, China had approximately 744 million telephone subscribers, 350 million with fixed line connections and 393 million mobile phone subscribers.

The six largest telecom operators in China are:

- China Telecom – operating fixed network, wireless local connections and PHS access.
- China Netcom – operating fixed network, wireless local connections and PHS access.
- China Mobile – operating a GSM network.
- China Unicom – the only operating company that offers the full range of services, operating GSM, CDMA and a fixed network.
- China Satcom – offering communications,

broadcasting and other areas of satellite communications.

- China Tie Tong - operating the communication services that support the rail network.

FINANCIAL SERVICE INDUSTRIES
Finance Industry

Finance is at the core of a modern economy. In the 1990s, China's financial industry developed through market-based reforms; opening its markets to foreign participation and leading to an increasingly competitive and innovative financial sector.

By the end of October 2005, there were more than 30,000 banking and financial institutions and organisations operating in China. These include 3 policy banks, 4 state-owned commercial banks, 13 share system commercial banks, 115 urban commercial banks, 626 urban credit co-operatives, 30,438 rural credit co-operatives, 57 rural co-operative (commercial) banks, 238 foreign capital banking institutions, 4 financial asset management companies, 59 trust and investment companies, 74 enterprise groups and financial affairs companies, 12 finance leasing companies,

5 automotive finance companies and many rural and urban postal savings institutions. At the same time, the total sum of the capital fund of RMB, foreign currency banking and financial institutions in China reached RMB36.2 trillion, a 19.2% increase from the first half of 2005. Within this figure, banking assets account for up to 90%, therefore assuming the most important position in the financial sector.

Foreign capital banks are increasing their foothold

in China day by day. By the end of October 2005, the total assets of foreign capital banks amounted to $84.5billion US dollars, around 2% of the total sum of the assets of all the financial institutions in the Chinese banking industry. The total RMB assets of foreign capital banks have exceeded 100 billion in the few years in which RMB business was opened. In the last few years, the Chinese banking industry has attracted many foreign investors and succeeded in opening up significant international industry.

Stock-based commercial banks have actively sought international investors to match their own strategic aspirations. Five out of the thirteen stock-based commercial banks have already attracted international investors. They are Shanghai Pudong Development Bank, the China Industrial Bank, Shenzhen Development Bank, China Everbright Bank and the China Minsheng Banking Corporation Limited. The Huaxia Bank has made important progress in attracting qualified foreign strategy investors. The Bohai Bank, which is under development, has carefully chosen a number of international capital banking partners as its founder members. Seven urban commercial banks: the Beijing, Shanghai, Nanjing, Xian, Jinan, Hangzhou and Nanchong urban commercial banks, have also successfully found strategic foreign investors.

The Banking System in China

The Chinese government has continued to prioritise the creation of a modern banking system – enabling them to strengthen their financial and economic control over the country. The system has repeatedly been modernised to comply with international standards. Meanwhile, the role of the central bank has been strengthened and policy-orientated lending has been separated from business lending.

The Central Bank and the Bank Regulators

In 2003, the central bank - the People's Bank of China (PBOC) was separated into two sections: the PBOC and China's Bank Regulatory Commission. The PBOC now operates as China's Central Bank and it is under the auspices of the State Council. The PBOC operates independently, but reports its decisions to the State Council. All financial operations are regulated by The Bank Regulatory Commission.

China's specialised banks have previously primarily dealt with commercial lending and low-interest, long-term loans made to businesses. In 1994 however, the Chinese government announced significant changes to the banking system. Under these reforms, the four major specialised banks: the Industrial and Commercial Bank of China, Bank of China, the Agricultural Bank of China and the Construction Bank of China, became purely commercial entities. They can now operate as individual profit centres and can offer a full portfolio of services. China recently restructured the share holding of the four wholly state-owned commercial banks to allow for partial international ownership.

In addition to these big four, there are another 104 commercial banks and a large number of co-operatives based across the country. The three policy banks are the China Development Bank, the Import-Export Bank of China and the Agricultural Development bank of China.

Insurance Industry

China has broken free from the long-term monopolisation of its insurance market by a single insurance company - the People's Insurance Company of China (PICC) - a conglomerate of the China Pacific Insurance Company (CPIC) and the Ping An Insurance Company of China (Ping An). There are now 52 insurance companies across China. Currently, the four largest insurance companies - PICC, the Chinalife Insurance Company, Ping An and CPIC dominate, possessing 96% of China's insurance market. Within this figure, Chinalife, a state-owned and exclusive investment insurance company, represents 70% of China's insurance market. Chinalife has 77% of market within life insurance, whilst PICC has 78% market share within property insurance and 82% of the automotive insurance market.

In September 1992, the People's Bank of China

authorised the American International Insurance Company - part of the American International Group Inc. - to set up a branch office in Shanghai, becoming the first foreign capital insurance company to enter the Chinese insurance market. To date, there are 32 joint venture branch offices.

Stock Exchange

On 19th December 1990, the Shanghai Stock Exchange was officially opened followed by the Shenzhen Stock Exchange on 3rd July 1991. The opening of these two stock exchanges marked

the beginning of stock trading in mainland China. China's reform of the share structure of listed companies in 2005 has led to improved liquidity in the domestic stock markets. These reforms have also significantly enhanced corporate governance.

Shanghai Stock Exchange – This Exchange is the prime market in mainland China. It assumes a market leading position in terms of the number of listed companies, stocks, market value, total circulating market value, total number of stock transactions, business volume of shares and government loans and by many other measures.

Shenzhen Stock Exchange – In the past 14 years, with the help of modern technology, Shenzhen, a new city, has successfully built a stock exchange which is available to the entire country. During this time, the Shenzhen Stock Exchange has raised approximately 365.8 thousand million RMB for its listed companies, and this has had a significant impact on both the financial and business sectors. From May 2004, the Shenzhen Stock Exchange has established a platform, within the main base of the stock market, for small and medium-sized business, similar to AIM on the London Stock Exchange.

TOURISM

China has multiplicitous opportunities for tourism with its high mountains, picturesque rivers and streams; rich and colourful folk culture, varied customs and traditions, unusual animals and plants and countless famous historical sites. In addition, there is a vast array of dramas and operas, music, dance and world famous cuisine. As a result, huge numbers of national and international tourists are attracted to China each year. China has one of the fastest growing tourist markets in the world.

According to the preliminary calculations of the World Travel and Tourism Council – the WTTC, China's travel and tourism industry should continue to increase by over 10% year on year over the next ten years. China is set to become the world's 4th largest economic centre for tourism. In addition, based on predictions from the World Tourism Organisation, by 2020, China will become the world's largest tourist destination.

As China's civil aviation, railways, inland water ways and motorway network are developing rapidly, the availability of convenient travel connections for national and international tourists are increasing. To cater for the differing levels of tourist requirements, a large number of hotels have been newly built, refurbished and enlarged giving a total of approximately 8,880 starred hotels throughout China.

MEDIA

China's media mirrors many of the changes occurring in China. Under the noticeably more relaxed regime set by the government, there exists a vibrancy and diversity in China's media where surprisingly open discussion of state policy and social issues now take place.

Talk radio is an example of this phenomenon giving ordinary people the opportunity to address their peers and even to the authorities regarding topical issues.

China's economic development and educational advancement have led to greater literacy, which in turn, is a major contributing factor driving China's media market to such dynamic expansion and diversification. Other factors include:

- increased contact with the West;
- greater commercial competition in the media market;
- receding government involvement in the media;

- new communication technologies;
- improved professional training for journalists;
- less government ideological dogma.

Of these elements, intense competition in the market, perhaps, plays the most important role. There are now over 2,000 newspapers, 9,000 magazines titles; over 125 million households with access to cable television, 1.22 million households in 30 cities with access to digital cable television. From just 12 television and 93 radio channels in 1965, China currently has 352 television stations and 273 radio stations with coverage of 94.6% and 93.3% of the population respectively. Since China Mobile started transmitting television programmes over its network in 2005, more than 150,000 people have subscribed to the service. The fastest growing forms of news casting are SMS messages, mobile reports and WAP sites.

Key organisations

The news agency **Xinhua** and the **People's Daily** are the two most important print media organisations. Whilst they have experienced constant and complicated reforms in recent years, they traditionally had the status of government ministries. Xinhua employs more than 10,000 people and has 107 bureaus worldwide. It is predominantly responsible for the collection and the dispensing of news information overseas, consequently, most of the newspapers rely on Xinhua feeds to fill their pages. As well as a news agency, Xinhua also has a stable of more than 20 newspaper and a dozen magazine titles of its own.

China's televsion industry has become a complete system with high-tech programme production, transmission and coverage. **Chinese Central Television (CCTV)** is the country's only national network, which also employs 10,000 people. It produces its own news broadcasts three times a day and has a monopoly on the purchase of programming from overseas. Shanghai is the biggest trading platform for television programmes in Asia.

China National Radio is China's official radio station. It has 9 channels broadcasting a total of 200 hours per day. At the same time, every province, region and municipality has its own local radio stations. **China Radio International (CRI)** is the only state-level radio station targeting overseas listeners.

Since entering the WTO, the trend within China's media has been to form inter-media alliances and trans-media operations over multiple platforms to compete with the challenges from powerful overseas media groups. **The China Radio, Film and Television Group** was founded in 2001. It integrated the resources to become China's biggest and strongest multi-media group.

EDUCATION

Chinese people have traditionally valued education and have great respect for teachers. The modern Chinese education system was established about a hundred years ago but initially developed quite slowly due to the semi-colonial and semi-feudal nature of Chinese society.

China's Educational System

• Infant Education

Pre-school education is for three to five year olds and takes place in nursery schools and kindergartens.

• Primary and Secondary Education

This is divided into three stages - primary, middle and senior schools with a total of 12 years of education. Primary and middle school education makes up the compulsory education stages. Primary education is for 6 to 11 year-olds, usually run by local educational authorities and some by independent organisations and individuals. Primary schools are for five or more often, six years. Secondary education is provided for 12-17 year-olds, conducted by local governments or business organisations. After three years of middle school education, students either enter another three years of senior school or three to five years at a vocational high school.

• Further Education

Further education consists of vocational, undergraduate, postgraduate and doctoral studies. In recent years, the number of privately-run colleges and universities has increased, to accommodate the increasing demand for further education.

SOCIAL WELFARE

Since 1998, China has adopted a 'two guarantees' policy. One is for the unemployed and the other is for retired people. A number of governmental insurance policies for different sections of the population are being implemented, for example:

- The Old-Age Insurance System
- The Medical Insurance System
- The Unemployment Insurance System
- Employment Injury Insurance
- The Birth Insurance System
- The Minimum Living Standard Security System
- The Social Welfare System
- The Special Care and Placement System
- The Natural Disaster Relief System
- The Social Mutual Help System

active 英中
创易
anglo chinese communications

Chapter 4

Understanding
the Chinese Psyche and
Building a Business Rapport

China is a vast country and making generalisations could be costly in a business environment. It is important to remember that China has evolved over 5,000 years of complex history and been subject to a diverse range of profound social and cultural influences. Even modern-day China battles with numerous constraints and pressures such as:

- The vast geographical area
- Highly regulated and centralised government policies
- The accelerating spread of urbanisation and globalisation
- A continuously evolving technological backdrop
- Environmental concerns

China as an emerging market is undoubtedly going through a complex transitional period. There are many opposing pressures at play between conflicting social and business environments:

- Central versus regional
- Global versus national versus local
- Urban versus rural
- New versus old
- Modern versus traditional
- Western versus Chinese

China has become a hot topic in the Western business community. It presents the world with many business opportunities and yet its challenges can be difficult to manage. Overcoming the language barrier is only part of the issue. The greatest challenge for the Western businessperson is in developing a real understanding of cultural differences: the implications behind body language; reading between the lines adjusting to particular situations and a strikingly different social environment. If you are equipped with some understanding of the Chinese business mentality and psyche on the following issues, the challenges can hopefully be turned to your advantage. At the very least, you will know where you stand!

Collectiveness

China, like many other Asian countries, has a collectivist culture. Its society places great emphasis on its groups and thinks more in terms of 'we' than 'I'. China bears significant distinctive features of collectivist cultures: harmony and loyalty within a group are very important and should always be maintained. This means that confrontation is avoided at all cost - subtle expressions or phrases are used to describe a disagreement or negative statement instead of saying 'no'. The relationship between employer and employee or business partners is based on trust, harmony and a deep understanding of moral values. The achievement, pride of the company and the group are far more important than those of the individual. It is important to ensure that you are aware of this deep-set feeling in any business dealings with Chinese people.

Patriotism

China's history is composed of numerous instances of invasion and colonisation by various countries and it has contributed to significant unrest. In recent decades, Mao's policy to rule China in isolation produced a deeper chasm between China and the Western world. As a result of its chequered history, patriotism is generally strong throughout China. Chinese people were at one time very conscious of being judged by their own country-folk for not being openly patriotic, and some will still express distrust when faced with unfamiliar Westerners. Hopefully, you will find that the atmosphere is far more relaxed these days. The Chinese increasingly enjoy Western influences in both business and culture, however, patriotism is still deep-rooted in the mind of the nation. It

is unwise to criticise China in any way - even the government - in small talk. It can be detrimental to the atmosphere and generates very negative vibes. In this case, the well known mantra still applies - "Don't ever be tempted to stand between the people and their country". It is rather like talking about one's own spouse: it is perfectly acceptable for a Chinese person to criticise their

own country, but it is just not the same for you to do so.

Hierarchy

Confucianism runs deeper than that most people are aware of. One of its teachings is a strong hierarchical system which most rulers have used in China's history to control the people. Nowadays, everyone has a social rank in the Chinese 'management' culture, and all are expected to know where they fit into the hierarchy and to behave accordingly.

There are diverse unspoken requirements in which hierarchy is continually reaffirmed in Chinese management culture. For example, hierarchy is very clear when entering a business meeting with a group of people. The highest-ranking person should be given the priority to enter the room, the lift and any other method of entry. They should then be followed by the most senior member of the Chinese party. However, guests should also be given priority, and seniority in age be considered. When the order is not clearly defined then a great deal of time could be lavished on observing this protocol.

Furthermore, hierarchy also determines introductions in meetings and seating arrangements at banquets. Therefore it is very important for you to ascertain where your counterparts fit into their hierarchy and then treat them accordingly.

Likewise, you need to understand your position within your hierarchy and your status in relation to your Chinese counterparts. If you are of a lower status in relationship to the person you are meeting, keep in mind that you will be expected to show respect to your higher status counterpart. If you are in a higher position than those around you, you are expected to live up to your status by being more reserved. Take the time to prepare for this and you will ensure that your trip runs as effectively as possible.

Mao Tse Tung's famous saying is that "The individual is subordinate to the organisation. The minority is subordinate to the majority. The lower level is subordinate to the higher level." This quotation embodies the hierarchical nature of Chinese society and companies. It also explains why Chinese people tend to be orientated more towards groups than individuals and often do not like to take responsibility. In a similar manner this can result in a situation where people are reluctant to give an opinion before their peers as it might cause disrespect or loss of face.

Harmony

Apart from Confucius, Tao is another philosopher who has had significant influence on the Chinese psyche. According to Taoism, Qi (pronounced 'chee') is a universal energy composed of two polarities: the yin and the yang, therefore balance and harmony are greatly promoted throughout society and history. This extends to other following aspects of life. An acknowledgement of this will be beneficial during your travels.

'Guanxi'

'Guanxi' means 'relationship', 'connection' or

'contacts'. Developing a good relationship between people is the main priority in the Chinese business world and relationships should be continuously consolidated and nurtured. Even in the West, the Chinese word 'Guanxi' has become a commonly used term within the Anglo-Chinese business community. Unlike in Western business culture, in China people believe in developing a relationship with a prospective business partner before they do busi-

ness. Historically in a centralised bureaucratic state, the use of personal contacts was the only way to get things done. Guanxi therefore has been considered as an effective alternative to a commercial and legal system. In China where the latter can be relatively weak the need to rely on Guanxi

continues to be strong. The members of a Guanxi network are expected to help each other at some point in time in a direct or indirect manner, contributing to a constructive cycle of relationships and development. Guanxi is key to opening doors - without Guanxi you will find it difficult to meet with senior managers/decision makers. It is difficult, in fact, near impossible, for a Western businessperson to connect with the right network of Guanxi within a short period of time. It is therefore essential that you enlist a dynamic and well connected person to look after this aspect of your business. As relationships are so highly regarded, the Chinese people will automatically honour them. Contacts introduced through a reliable and credible source will receive a friendly reception on first meeting and people often go out of their way to initiate connections. An individual with a widespread Guanxi network is typically referred to as powerful and resourceful but the reality must always live up to the reputation. You should aim to understand this and capitalise on the power it can create for your business.

'Face'

Face is a mark of personal dignity and is a core aspect of the Chinese mindset. The Chinese people are extremely sensitive with regard to gaining and maintaining face in all aspects of social and business life. Face is highly prized and can be given, lost, taken away or earned. 'Giving face' for example, can mean to express respect, show support or avoid embarrassing somebody. In a business environment, 'giving face' can also mean complimenting staff in front of their employer, or attending a business meeting dressed immaculately as a demonstration of respect. 'Face' is also linked with hierarchy i.e. recognising and valuing an individual's position or status, and behaving accordingly. The opposite of this - to 'lose face' - is used to describe an act of disrespect and may involve spoiling someone's business prospects. It is important to avoid being critical towards individuals in front of a crowd in the company of Chinese people - a quiet word will always be more warmly received. Even making fun of an individual in a good-natured, humorous way can be perceived as a sign of lack of respect, so be mindful of this. Equally, whilst giving face earns respect and loyalty, over-use suggests insincerity, so be careful how you use it!

Modesty

Whilst dealing with your Chinese counterparts or your employees either socially or in business, you may find them very modest. People are often shy when receiving compliments, or instead, simply reject them to disguise their embarrassment. It is not that they don't think they deserve the compliments; it is because they are unable to articulate the most appropriate modest reply. It is regarded as ill mannered and arrogant to accept a compliment or boast about it, because in Chinese culture, arrogance is a route to failure. Modesty can also be used before accepting a task or during an interview, as it is the Chinese way to avoid expressing themselves inappropriately. All of these attitudes are rooted in the Confucius teaching, "A superior man should be modest in his speech, but excel in his actions".

Understanding the Chinese psyche and striking a business rapport clearly requires an abundance of common sense and business tactics. If you are equipped with great communication skills, an attitude to adapt, an open mind and a flexible and diplomatic approach, you will have a great chance of success in China. Hopefully, this guide will provide you with a good grounding for your thriving business future!

active 英中
anglo chinese communications 创易

Chapter 5

Business and Social Etiquette

Having understood a little about the Chinese psyche, we can now go on to look at how this impacts on contemporary Chinese social and business etiquette. Fortunately in today's modern China, people are not as rigid in their interpretation of this etiquette. The extent of its importance depends on the type of company you are dealing with and your counterpart's personal background. Generally speaking, governmental or state-owned organisations tend to be more hierarchical and therefore more collective in their decision-making. In this context, certain business etiquette has to be followed more strictly. On the other hand, in businesses such as joint ventures and private enterprises, the situation is likely to be far more relaxed. The same also goes for the younger generation of Chinese business people. Many of them will have returned to China from an overseas education and will have almost certainly adapted to a Westernised approach to business.

Below are a few tips that will help you navigate your business travel to China!

Dress Code and Clothing

Whilst suits and ties are not always the requisite

dress code for your Chinese host (especially in a more industrial environment) this dress code is expected from a Westerner at meetings. It goes without saying that a smart business appearance would give you extra confidence in an unfamiliar country, and would also imply that you have a level of respect for your host. It is easier for men; a couple of suits and a few shirts would cover more

or less all eventualities and dispensing with ties in meetings is a good way to relax the atmosphere. However, whilst it can be slightly trickier for the ladies, generally speaking, a few smart suits and layered business wear would be suitable. It is important to be mindful of the fact that too much exposure can be embarrassing and uncomfortable for Chinese men, (although it doesn't mean that they don't find it attractive!)

It is also important to be prepared for evening functions, but luckily you don't tend to need to dress up. The early Chinese dinners (about 6pm) normally take place straight after the afternoon meetings and don't require extra outfits. The most formal 'black tie do's' enjoyed in the West are fairly rare in China. Over the Chinese New Year, the traditional 'retro' style becomes quite popular. Comfortable shoes are recommended as a one day schedule could comprise of a series of meetings, a visit to the Great Wall of China and a lavish banquet in the evening!

It is important to note that the weather changes dramatically from one province to the other and because of the different build of the local men and women and their taste, it may be difficult to find what you want to wear from the local shops. It is also advisable to bring suitable attire to take into account the differing climatic conditions that prevail throughout China.

Business Card Exchange

The exchange of business cards is a relatively new business tradition. It has only become popular in recent decades as the economic structure in China has evolved. The card is usually presented with two hands and a slight forward bow. Although this might seem a little awkward at first - particularly in a social environment like a cocktail party -

it is important to follow this etiquette to begin to build mutual respect between you and your Chinese counterpart and form the basis of a trusting business relationship.

Business Cards: Getting It Right

Even though a business card only contains a handful of words, it should never be under-estimated!

A basic business card carries your company name, your personal name, the all-important job title as well as an ever increasing number of contact details. Without any common ground in terms of

the Chinese language, this little card is of paramount importance in making a positive impression on your new associate so that they can remember who you are for later dealings.

Having the card in Chinese should be your most important preparation for your trip to China. The Chinese language is a pictorial language; each character has a meaning or a set of meanings and combining characters can produce new connotations. In English, you wouldn't want to give yourself a first name of 'Don' when you have a surname of 'Key', and a similar situation could happen in Chinese too! It is important to note that some words have negative implications attached to them. It is a good idea therefore to always compile a series of positive words to convey an upbeat profile.

Another powerful feature of the business card is the job title. With China's historically hierarchal background in mind, it is important not to undersell yourself. Perhaps it is reflective of the business world in general, but certainly in China people prefer to speak to decision-makers. As different companies have varying ways of structuring and assigning job titles, you must ensure that your Chinese associates understand the seniority of your position in relation to business decision-making. At the same time, you must also be careful that your position does not sound in any way superior to your boss. Many Western titles would be completely new to the Chinese due to the international differences in company structure. It is sensible to employ a little creativity in translating the titles to evoke a full understanding of what each individual does and his/her seniority in the company.

Gift Giving

It is a well-established Chinese tradition to exchange gifts with visitors, especially during the first visit. Gift-giving is a ritual that plays an important part in any business dealings. Whom to give to, what to give and when to give are all im-

portant points of consideration. As mentioned, formal business etiquette has to be adapted to the organisation/company or the person you are dealing with. A strict procedure sometimes has to be adopted according to the circumstances. For example, if your counterpart works in a government department, the timing and the value of the presents is better to be ascertained at a lower level (between the assistants), in order that protocol is suitably followed and no-one loses face. Normally, the highest valued gift should be presented to the key person, i.e. the decision maker and/or the highest ranked official. Other relevant people should also be considered. To avoid missing anyone out, extra gifts should be prepared just in case. The value of the gifts should be relatively moderate as corruption is a sensitive issue at Chinese government level. The most popular gift would be unfamiliar to the Chinese people, representative of your own country and evocative of a meaningful story or positive message. A good choice could serve as an ice-breaker, symbolising a good basis for the ongoing relationship between the two companies/countries. Apart from meaningful gifts, a popular gift would be something that the receiver can display in the office or at home. Initiating business dealings with a Western company in China is still seen as a sign of prestige; it elevates a company's success, credibility and reputation.

When you meet each other for the first time, a gift exchange normally takes place almost immediately. It could also be part of a contract signing ceremony – normally at the end to celebrate this milestone. The Chinese are often too shy or feel that it would be impolite to unwrap the present but they would be quite happy to do so if prompted - curiosity is a borderless impulse!

Remember to bring some small souvenirs from your own country. Warm and generous hospitality will be given from the top management to the junior staff. It is not appropriate to give tips or money - small gifts will be always remembered.

Suitably Addressing your Chinese Counterpart

In contrast to Western names, Chinese names are read out in reverse order – the family name is followed by the first name.

The Chinese have a different custom for calling each other by their names. An individual who is above a certain age and social status will commonly not be addressed by their given name. There is no standard rule as to how to address your Chinese contact in a polite, appropriate yet friendly way. It goes without saying though that you should aim to demonstrate your respect to their age and social status, and to ensure that it is appropriate to the social situation and custom of the country. To avoid complications, it is safest for a Westerner to address a Chinese contact by their surname such as 'Mr. Wang', 'Dr. Ma' or 'Madam Yu'. But for convenience and to demonstrate your desire to build a closer relationship, it can be shortened to 'Wang' or 'Ma' if appropriate. However, it is the norm to address the government officials or people with senior positions by

their rank as well as their name e.g. 'Chairman Li, General Manager Zhang'. But remember, never add 'deputy' to their title, even if they are. Using rank to represent a person's status is especially important between the Chinese as it is seen to show respect and 'give face', conversely, if used inappropriately, this can create loss of face. In a less formal environment, to avoid addressing each other by name, people generally use a work title such as 'Engineer Wang' or 'Accountant Ma'. 'Teacher Zhang' and their surname can often be heard between new acquaintances to demonstrate courtesy and respect. It originates from the teachings of Confucius: if three people are walking together, at least one of them can be my teacher. Between friendly colleagues, the Chinese would call each other 'old Wang', 'little Ma'. For a non-Chinese speaking Westerner, addressing each other may be the only way of establishing communication with their Chinese counterpart. It sounds complicated, but don't forget, you can always ask the person directly or seek assistance from your interpreter.

Having said all that, China is changing and becoming more and more influenced by the Western business etiquette. The younger Chinese people often give themselves an English name for fun or simply for easier pronunciation by the Westerners. These English first names are usually employed solely for practical use, they are not official, and often none of their Chinese colleagues would be aware of them. If you need to mention this person to the others, you may also have to get the spelling of their Chinese name.

Banquets in China

To welcome Western friends from afar, banquets are often hosted at lavish restaurants. Typical banquets consist of many courses, often with exotic delicacies not usually eaten in the West. Politeness decrees that you should at least taste the food on offer - especially if you are the guest of honour.

Deciding a table plan could take up a few minutes. The seats that face the door are regarded as the top seats, as such, this is where the two senior people from each party are seated. Guests are seated further away from the host in descending order of seniority, with the most junior having their back to the door. The interpreter is usually placed

between guests who cannot speak each other's languages. Don't worry too much about this protocol – it is easier to let the Chinese party arrange it, and simply follow their lead.

It is usual for a Chinese host to serve food to the guest. If you are the host you should also try to serve your guest. In any case, you will need to join in the process of serving or being served. It is not an option to hide in the background!

Never arrive late for a meal - Chinese people often arrive early. They also tend to leave en masse as soon as the last dish has been eaten. Await the lead from your Chinese counterpart - Chinese hosts make it clear when the gathering is finished.

Typically in China, meals are eaten earlier than in the West. Lunch is served from midday and dinner from around 6.00p.m.

There are no hard and fast rules for table manners – it's more about fitting in. If in doubt, follow your host's example. Chinese people don't mind if you ask for knives and folks, though, generally only a spoon is available in a Chinese restaurant. Be mindful that Chinese people tend to be quite amused and amazed when seeing a Westerner using chopsticks well – it may be worth having a practice before your trip! One gaffe to avoid - do not leave your chopsticks pointing into the bowl - place them horizontally on the rest provided.

Payment for the banquet is usually made by the 'inviter'. A welcome banquet is usually hosted by the Chinese party, a 'thank you' banquet is reciprocated by the Western visitors. For informal meals, the Chinese would normally offer to settle the bill, but offering to take turns is always regarded as courteous. Splitting the bill has become fashionable amongst the younger generation but it is not a general custom in China.

Toasts

Frequent toasts are standard either with locally produced wine or 'Bai Jiu' (strong spirit), but 'Pi Jiu' (beer) is also widely drunk and it is perfectly acceptable to order one instead, especially when China's beer has an excellent reputation amongst Westerners!

The head of each party is expected to give a speech and a toast using Chinese wines is part of the occasion. Some Western people become very popular among the Chinese people because of their capacity to drink Chinese wine! To some, it is a sign of being approachable and agreeable. The toasting etiquette can be overwhelming and generally speaking it is more prevalent in the North-West of China. In these situations, the host may relentlessly persuade you to drink more. To let your host down is to be avoided at all costs; it is therefore advisable to prepare a good excuse in advance!

Speeches

On many occasions during your trip you may be invited to give a speech e.g. the opening of a toast at a banquet; the opening proceedings of a contract signing ceremony or meeting your partner company's team for the first time. A speech is regarded as an honour for both the speaker and the audience. When making the speech, don't forget to emphasise the following key points:

- Love and respect for your host's country
- What a pleasure it is to build a friendship with the people you are visiting

- How you will benefit their organisation and ulti mately their country
- The fact that you are planning for the long term, not for immediate benefits
- The fact that the relationship you are building is based on mutually beneficial ground

Chapter 6

How to Communicate
Effectively with
Chinese People

Choosing the Most Suitable Communication Channel

The key challenge for any business arrangement between the UK and China is communication. Despite having a multitude of advanced technological tools at their disposal, businesspeople from China and the West are still frustrated by the constraints of communication. There are many factors at play here - including distance, time difference, the unreliability of communication technology, the inability to communicate, or simply the reluctance of business partners to improve communication channels.

This chapter aims to provide some advice and information based on our team's knowledge to ensure that your experience is as positive as it can be.

Whilst Chinese companies employ communication channels that are similar to their Western counterparts (mobile phones, landlines, faxes, email, post and express mail), it is important to understand that they are often used in very different ways to the West.

Landlines and Mobile Phones

Make sure that you accumulate your key contacts' mobile telephone numbers at the outset of your dealings. Whilst a mobile phone is undoubtedly an essential tool of communication in the UK, they are used even more frequently and extensively in China with over 500 million mobile phone subscribers! Today's entrepreneurs simply cannot live without them. Chinese businesspeople will answer their mobiles whenever and wherever they are - in meetings, at the dinner table, on holiday or at a family gathering. Westerners are often offended when their Chinese counterparts

interrupt their meetings with mobile phone calls. However this cultural dissimilarity is as beneficial to UK businesses as it is frustrating - that phone call could well be yours when you are desperately trying to confirm last minute changes to a specification prior to production!

It is worth mentioning that it is not always free to receive phone calls on mobiles in China so not all companies will bear this cost for their staff. When dealing with lowered salaried staff you should be mindful of this, as there may be some reluctance

to provide their number for that reason. However, you will find that people are generally happy to give out their mobile phone numbers.

A Chinese landline is a particularly unreliable communication channel. Unlike a mobile phone it will not always be answered, especially at older or more conventional Chinese organisations. If there is no-one in the office, the phone could ring forever without an answer phone kicking in or the switchboard operator reconnecting with your call! Some companies do have individual lines to each office but in most cases it is entirely down to luck whether you can reach anyone. Communicating in office hours from another country is complicated further by the time difference. For easier communication, you may find that your Chinese colleagues are happy to give you their mobile number as well as their home number. In many cases, they will invite you to call them at any time of day as your call is long distance and therefore important. However, if you are willing to reciprocate, make sure they realise the time difference – unless you are happy to receive calls in the early hours!

Fax and Email

Fax machines continue to be very popular in China for a variety of reasons. Firstly, a fax provides proof of a document's origin and source; secondly, it offers fast and safe delivery to the end user (no computer viruses lurking there!); thirdly, writing

Chinese characters by hand is easier than typing on a computer keyboard and the final reason is that email connections are not always reliable or accessible. The only problem with communicating by fax is that they are not confidential. When a fax arrives at its destination it can be read by anybody within the office and it is therefore impossible to determine whether the intended reader has received your document. Therefore, before sending the document, it is advisable to make contact with the intended recipient to ensure that they are aware that the fax is about to be transmitted.

Today's business world relies on email as a fast and economical me-thod of communication. But while Western companies enjoy good email connections, the same cannot be assumed of all Chinese businesses. Progressive service-driven companies with forward-looking management will certainly have modern equipment, with all key staff members enjoying their own PCs and company email addresses. This, however, is unlikely to be the case with more traditional and manufacturing-based companies. Even if a business boasts a professional, modern website, it may not have an associated email address or it may only have a single generic address shared by many members of staff. Under these circumstances, many employees create a private email account for business use. Be aware however that these are often poorly maintained. For example, when the private email account has been filled with spam mail, the existing email account will be abandoned in favour of a new email address. Unfortunately, this new address is not often communicated to all genuine customers!

Post and Express Delivery Services

Unlike in the UK, the postal service in China is

largely an unreliable means of delivering a package or letter. It is safer to guarantee the delivery of your package by paying an extra charge for an express delivery. The charge for this method of delivery tends to be pretty reasonable, although sometimes you will find your important package has travelled via five buses, two tube lines and on the back of several bicycles! It does get there though!

In addition to the traditional methods of communication that we have all come to depend upon in recent times as described above, there is an increasing reliance on more modern techniques to keep in contact:

Messenger, Skype and SMS Text Messaging

Continuing technological innovation in telecommunications channels is playing an increasingly important role in people's social and business lives. In comparison with other methods of communication, they are cheaper, quicker and generally unobtrusive. They are very popular and especially favoured for communicating with overseas colleagues and business partners.

Face-to-Face Communication Versus Telephone Conferencing

Face-to-face communication is always the ideal approach to establishing and nurturing a business relationship. Equally, when language is a barrier, it might be better to convey your ideas and opinions to the interpreter by writing figures or drawing pictures on a flip chart. However, this is not always possible for long distance communications, and verbal interaction with your Chinese contact is the next best thing to maintain that personal connection. Whilst video conferencing is a relatively new concept in China, it is not difficult for your Chinese contacts to connect to your conference call through a line set up in the UK. It is important to ensure that a

sophisticated conference phone facility is set up so that the group can communicate effectively.

Language: Mandarin or Cantonese

The official language of China is Mandarin Chinese or Putonghua. It bases its phonology on the Beijing dialect, although it also takes some elements from other sources. It is taught and used in schools, universities and standard broadcasts. Almost all people who have received some education at school in China can at least speak some Mandarin. Since 1997, many Hong Kong schools have been teaching in Mandarin.

There are, however, many varying dialects in this vast country. Among these, Cantonese is the best known and the most extensively spoken outside of China. Cantonese originates from, and is spoken by the people from the Guangdong/Guangxi region, as well as people from Hong Kong and Chinese immigrants all over the world. Mandarin sounds completely different from Cantonese and, interestingly, most people who use Mandarin wouldn't be able to readily understand a Cantonese speaker.

There is a slight complication relating to the written Chinese as there are two types of Chinese characters: simplified and traditional. The simplified version is, as the name suggests, a simplified form of the traditional Chinese characters and it has been developed gradually since 1949 when China established its communist government. The traditional version is, however, still used by Chinese people overseas. In general, Mandarin with simplified Chinese characters should be employed for communicating with a mainland Chinese audience.

There are many thousands of Chinese characters. However, unlike European languages, there is no link between written and spoken Chinese. To increase the literacy level and to hope that children associate characters with spoken words that they already know, Pinyin (or Hanyu Pinyin) was approved in 1958 and adopted in 1979.

Interpreting and Translation

Translating the language verbally is usually referred to as interpreting. Depending on the scale of the event, there are two styles of interpreting to choose from - 'consecutive' and 'simultaneous'.

Simultaneous interpreting is often used for large seminars and conferences. For smaller business meetings, consecutive interpreting is more appropriate and the quality of the interpretation can be controlled better.

When doing business in China, establishing a contact to act as an intermediary is important. This brings with it multiple benefits. They can act as a reference, be your interpreter and navigate you through the bureaucracy, legal system and local business networks. However, as your business relationship will be predominantly in the hands of your interpreter, it is crucial that you choose someone that you can trust completely in relation to their loyalty and competency.

At the negotiation table, your interpreter's role becomes even more important. Once the channels of effective communication and trust have been developed between you and the interpreter, you can benefit in many ways. Your interpreter can become your negotiation partner, helping to steer the conversation in the direction you want it to go. They can pick up messages beyond the language; identify the relationships within the opposite party and make an accurate judgement on who the real decision maker is. While the words are being interpreted you can sit back and observe, and then compare notes with your interpreter after the meeting.

How to Work with an Interpreter
Who makes the arrangements for an interpreter? Normally the Western visitor to China relies on their Chinese counterpart to provide an interpreter. However it is recommended that you have your own interpreter available for initial and important meetings.

Where do you find an interpreter? There are many translation agencies in China that provide interpreting services, but standards can vary considerably. A recommendation through a reliable source may prove to be the best way, so talk to your business contacts or friends.

Briefing your interpreter: Ideally it is important to use someone you know well and to brief them fully beforehand. In any case it makes sense to involve your interpreter in your pre-meeting arrangements. Ensure that your interpreter understands what you are aiming to achieve.

Clarity is essential: Speak in manageable sentences, at an even pace. Do not ramble! Conversely, do not speak in short phrases and unfinished sentences, as your interpreter may find it impossible to translate the meaning if you have left a sentence incomplete. Try to write down numbers wherever possible, as large numbers can be tricky to interpret in Chinese. Avoid the use of jargon and finally, ensure that any key terminology that may be used during the course of the meeting is discussed and understood in advance of the meeting.

Cross checking: Even with a good interpreter, there is still scope for misunderstanding. By repeating important points and cross-referencing crucial issues, this will ensure that the key messages and outcomes will be communicated effectively.

Observe body language when your words are being interpreted: This is a good opportunity to make your own judgement on who might be the decision-maker and influencer.

Time: Remember that the need to interpret speeches and presentations will effectively cut your speaking time in half.

Humour: It is best to avoid jokes and witticisms. Remember, when doing business you are representing your company so always keep dealings at a professional level. This is not because the Chinese are humourless but instead that jokes may be lost in translation and hence be redundant.

Making Your Presentation Powerful
Chinese, Everything in Chinese!

Don't assume that English is a business language used throughout the world. Your direct contacts in China may speak brilliant English, but the decision makers, their bosses or the Board of Directors may not understand or be too busy to have the time and patience to read the documents in English. Having your company brochure, presentation and any relevant handouts translated into Chinese is essential in order to maximise the potential of your business trip.

Knowing your Audience and their Needs

Make sure you have done your homework before doing business in China. The Chinese people plan meticulously and will know your business and possibly you inside out. Conducting some research prior to your meeting can help you to understand your audience and the decision makers amongst them far better. Based on the information you gather about their business issues and their local, national and international market environment will make your presentation more targeted.

Give Them What They Want and More!

Many forward-thinking Chinese companies use PowerPoint. Their presentation is usually full of well-researched data and sophisticated graphics. The same is expected from a Western company.

If the presentation is designed to provide your audience with a profile of your company, then the Chinese audience would want to know the size of your organisation, the number of staff employed and if your client base is made up of established brands

within the marketplace. If your presentation can include humorous and more visual illustrations, it is more likely to retain their interest.

International information and your analysis can be very interesting to the Chinese audience. Because of the language barrier and limited resources, many Chinese companies may not be well equipped to absorb in-depth facts and figures globally. Equally, case studies of similar natured projects that took place in another country are always very popular.

Blow Your Own Trumpet and Impress!
A presentation stands for way more than a few slides - your Chinese counterpart will want to test out your confidence and technical capability level. The level of preparation you have put into the presentation can demonstrate the level of importance you ascribe to this project. Be prepared to blow your own trumpet!! Your company may be a leading international player in its industry, but you may have to assume that the Chinese people may have never heard of you! So do articulate your ambition, your capabilities, your track record and, most importantly, what you can

achieve for their organisation.

Chinese-Style Networking

As relationships are high on the agenda, Chinese businesspeople are experts at networking and most business deals are struck through social and business networking events.

The Food Culture

The Chinese people are proud of their food culture. Entertainment by banquet is one of the most common and popular ways of celebrating this culture. Frequent dinner entertainment is a way of life for a businessperson. It is regarded as a very important networking opportunity. A group of local like-minded associates often gather together and talk with each other over dinner, exchanging industry news and trading information. Many people agree that most of their opportunities are created through these lunches and dinners. Before important festivals such as the Chinese New Year, businesspeople will hardly ever have time for their own families! Gifts are given on these occasions but the participants also recognise that spending time with people is of more importance. Banqueting is perhaps the most popular form of networking and drinking Chinese rice wine and endless toasting is inevitable! (see more information in Chapter 5).

Karaoke

The Chinese have adopted the Japanese musical invention 'karaoke' and it has become hugely popular. In fact, it has now become the most

popular entertainment form amongst Chinese people. There are huge entertainment complexes throughout China that are open 24 hours a day. Private singing rooms are available with designated waiters/waitresses employed to be at your service throughout the night. These venues are equipped with karaoke facilities and you will be served with drinks and fruit. After a few drinks and some 'singing' (in the loosest possible sense of the word!!), an informal atmosphere is created. You may find that once you have sung your first song, you may want to develop your career as a singer! Lasting friendships are formed through the camaraderie developed throughout the evening.

Spas and Beauty Parlours

Whilst corporate hospitality may not exist at football clubs or at the theatre in China,

pampering valued customers at Spas and Beauty Parlours certainly takes place throughout the country. It depends on where you visit, but clean and luxurious places can easily be found through word-of-mouth. Men and women are separate when experiencing the spa treatments but everyone can meet up in their pyjamas (provided by the parlour!) for a good meal or further treatments such as reflexology or massage. These activities are very popular amongst close associates and friends, but it may be too intimate for you to enjoy with your new Chinese colleagues. In which case, a simple reflexology treatment or a head massage could help with your jetlag and provide the opportunity for a good bonding session with your Chinese counterparts.

Golfing and Other Clubs

An increasing number of Chinese businesspeople are taking up golf, although it is currently considered to be a very expensive, elitist sport. Their enthusiasm for networking is the same as in the West, although their golfing ability is not quite up to par! Other than golf, there are many private clubs and social circles emerging based around exclusive hobbies, engaged in by the more economically affluent population, such as diving or sports cars.

MBA and Special Training Classes

Education is always high on the agenda in China. 'Recharging your batteries' for senior management has become a widespread phenomenon. Different training courses to accommodate this

trend are designed by well-known universities or large corporate organisations from all over the world. The courses have become a breeding ground for networking at a high level. Despite the huge costs associated with enrolling on such courses, the huge networking values and opportunities to be derived far outweigh any monetary concerns.

Top Ten Business Discussion Topics:
- General business trends and patterns
- New government policies on business
- New business development ideas and opportunities
- News and gossip on new and existing businesses
- Collaboration opportunities
- Evaluation of return on investment
- Public relations – new 'guanxi' created
- Estates and properties
- International and domestic stock market
- Premium business entertainment, e.g. overseas travel, golf, tennis, new clubs

active 英中
anglo chinese communications
创
易

Chapter 7

Background
Information to Help the
Conversation Flow!

In China, people prefer to get to know their business contacts before doing business with them. Therefore, a round of social occasions would be recommended to help everyone get to know each other better. Many non-Chinese speaking international businesspeople gather a circle of Chinese friends around them; these people will be invaluable if they are intuitive and socially adept. Under normal circumstances,

there will always be English speakers in a business environment. However, talking about the weather and the traffic won't be enough to develop a fledgling relationship. The more knowledge you have about China on the whole, the more common ground you will be able to find with your business associates and the better you will be able to make conversations flow, therefore deepening the relationship. Equally, showing your knowledge of China and an active interest in their country will make you a very popular guest and will help to lighten the atmosphere. Here are some useful facts about China:

Food in China

Dining is perhaps the most popular pastime and form of entertainment in China: all important and everyday festivals, occasions, gatherings and ceremonies involve a lot of eating! If you are doing business in China, it will not take you long to discover the importance of food in Chinese culture. Every lunch and dinner is treated with the utmost respect. A quick business lunch can easily expand into a huge feast, even if there is only a small number in your party! The enthusiasm for food itself is a huge topic at the table. People compare notes on the trendiest dish available at the moment, which new restaurant's food is value for money, or which new eating experience they have had. As a visitor, the host will not expect you to know everything about Chinese food, but it would be greatly appreciated if you are able to display some knowledge of the subject, because it shows that you have respect for them and an interest in their country.

China is a vast country with an extensive geography, diverse climate and a multitude of cultural differences. These, and many historical circumstances contributed to a broad and differing range of Chinese foods available in the country. There are generally four types of cuisine: the Northern plains - including Beijing; the fertile East - watered by the Yangtse River; the South, famous for the Cantonese cooking of the Guangdong Province; and the fecund West of Sichuan and the Hunan Provinces. Each type includes a range of different types of dish, the most renowned traditional categories are:

• Cantonese (Yue): From Guangzhou/Canton - the most famous with Westerners, as it is served in most of the Chinese restaurants overseas.

- Shandong (Lu): Often regarded as an everyday meal served in the Northern area in places such as Beijing and Shandong. Soy Sauce is an important ingredient.
- Sichuan (Chuan): Its distinctive taste is chilli, making it very hot and spicy. It is likely to be an interesting experience for fans of Indian food.
- Jiangsu (Su or Yang): Quite light in comparison with other Northern dishes, and with a sweet taste.

Other major types of cuisine include Fujian (Min), Hunan (Xiang), Zhejiang (Zhe) and Anhui (Hui) styles.

Other than the traditional meals, there are many new and unusual dishes appearing in the trendy restaurants in major cities. Their incredible array of ingredients can range from Western goat's cheese and potato chips to Chinese Soy Sauce and Sichuan chilli pepper. In addition, there is also a vast selection of foreign food available in China: Italian, French, Indian, Brazilian, Thai - to name but a few types. Western food can always be a good choice for taking your Chinese contacts out for a change.

Typical Chinese Dishes to Sample

- Peking Duck, Beijing （北京烤鸭）- Its authentic taste can't be found in any Chinese restaurant in the West.
- Chinese Hotpot, Mongolian （火锅）- A national dish to help to endure the harsh winters in the North.

- Steamed Pot, Yuannan （气锅）- A soup with a healthy mixture of meat and vegetables.
- Pork Stew （炖肉）- Mao Tse Tong's favourite dish, it is interpreted in many different ways throughout the country, but the basic ingredient is the same: pork belly. It looks fatty but tastes great.
- Spicy Fish Hotpot, Sichuan （水煮鱼）- A very stimulating experience if you have a strong

enough palate for chilli and Chinese pepper.

- Dim Sum, Guangdong (早茶) - It is as popular in China as in the Chinese restaurants throughout the world, it is worth comparing it to your own experience of the dish!

- Little Steamed Dumplings, Shanghai (小笼包) - A mouth-watering experience, worth queuing at the Nanxiang Restaurant for!

- Dumplings, Northern (饺子) - A typical dish for Chinese New Year's Eve, representing the union of the family.

- Hand-pulled Noodles, Northern (拉面) - This dish is more of an artistic display than a cookery process. Witnessing the production of the thread-like noodles is a true amazing experience.

Tea Culture

Made from camellia leaves, there are six major types of tea – Green, Black, Wulong, White, Scented and tightly pressed tea (sometimes called 'gunpowder' tea due to its colour and shape). Green Tea has the longest history and remains the most popular, enjoyed for its freshness and natural fragrance.   Famous green teas include Longjing (Dragon Well) from Hangzhou, Maofeng Tea from the Huangshan Mountain, Yinzhen (Silver Needle) Tea from the Junshan Mountain, Yunwu (Cloud and Mist) Tea from the Lushan Mountain, and Wulong from Fujian in the

Southeast of the country. Scented tea, made by mixing green tea with flower petals is unique to China. Sweet osmanthus, jasmine, rose, orchid and plum flowers are all available.

The Contribution of Chinese People to the World

- The Compass - Invented in China during the Qin dynasty (221-206 B.C.). In the 15th century, Zheng He made several ocean crossings using the compass.

- Paper – In 105 A.D., bark from the mulberry tree and bamboo fibres were blended with water and pounded to a pulp. Once dried it formed an excellent writing surface.

- Printing - Block printing is probably one of China's most significant inventions. This occurred during the Tang Dynasty sometime between the 4th and 7th centuries A.D.
- Gunpowder/fireworks – A mixture of saltpetre (potassium nitrate), sulphur, and powdered charcoal invented in the latter part of the Han dynasty, during 3rd century A.D. Mixing gunpowder with other elements that burn to give different colours led to the creation of the first ever fireworks. The above four inventions are the most well known contributions made by Chinese people to the world's development.
- Porcelain – In the 13th century, Marco Polo described the beauty of Chinese porcelain in

his book. It wasn't until the 18th century that it was successfully produced in Europe.

- Silk – One of the strongest natural fibres, stronger than steel, was obtained and woven from silk moth caterpillar cocoons.

- Trade Routes – transcontinental trade routes such as the 'Silk Road' which ran from Xi'an to Rome were developed.

- Seismograph – During the Han Dynasty, Emperor He's Royal Astronomer - Hang Chen was responsible for the invention of the seismograph to predict the strength and direction of earthquakes.

Sport in China

Given the background of Chinese modern history, sport has been strongly linked with politics and national pride, and the economy also plays a very important role in its development. Therefore, from generation to generation, the public's favourite sports have repeatedly changed according to these influences. The Chinese people's passion for sport is no different to that of any other country. Of course, a sport in which the Chinese people excel, especially at an international level, attracts more interest. Therefore, the Olympics is the most important sporting event, with other international tournaments that involve Chinese players (except football) attracting a tremendous following in China. Chinese sport has experienced its greatest period of development since the economic reforms were initiated in 1978. During this period, the more traditional sports such as martial arts, wrestling, chess and boat racing have been replaced by more Westernised activities. Many Chinese people now have the option of a variety of sports originating in different countries, and can even enjoy spectator sports such as watching the NBA competition on TV. Here are today's most popular sports in China:

Table Tennis

Also known as 'ping pong', this has always been a sport in which the Chinese people have excelled on an international stage since the 1960s. In 1971, the Chinese table tennis team invited the American table tennis team to visit the People's Republic of China. During this all expenses paid trip, significant bridges were built between the American and Chinese people in the sports arena. It is testament to the value of the sport in

China, that the US team were the first group of Americans allowed into China since 1949 when China was founded. This was coupled by an economic development, as during this trip, the US announced plans to remove a 20-year  embargo on trade with China. Table tennis is still one of the biggest amateur recreational sports in China today, with an estimated 200 million players.

Volleyball

Once again, sport became entwined with politics during the defeat of the Japanese women's volleyball team by the Chinese team in the 1981 World Championships. Although the political context was a period of significant modernisation in the country, this sporting victory spurred the nation on in a sense of national pride – previously only seen before the Cultural Revolution. Not only did they defeat China's traditional Asian rival Japan, but they also went on to win at the

Olympics and five consecutive world titles. China had previously held the embarrassing sporting label of 'the sick man of East Asia' – a label that was removed by this period of victory.

Badminton

Another sport in which the Chinese people excel is badminton. This means that it continues to be one of the most popular recreational sports in the country today. The Chinese team has achieved a

number of sporting victories including winning the World Championship, the England Open, the Sudirman Cup and many Olympic medals. Many Chinese people enjoy playing badminton in the open air, without a net or a court, meaning that it can be enjoyed by anyone at any time.

Basketball

There is a theory perpetuated by some historians that basketball originated in China as an evolution of the 'shouju' game. This was a street-based handball game with a circular net that was in existence way before basketball. Regardless of its origin, the sport has grown from strength to strength in China, and increased significantly in popularity since Chinese professional basketball player Yao Ming signed for Houston in 2002. Yao Ming was named a global ambassador for the Special Olympics World Games in 2007 and is one of the country's favourite athletes.

Football

Football is hugely popular in China and attracts more fans here than anywhere else in the world. Unlike China's other popular sports however, the Chinese people have not yet triumphed in football despite their best efforts. This means that international teams attract more interest than their national counterparts – in particular the teams in the English Premiership, the Italian Serie A and

the German Bundesliga. If a Chinese player signs for a particular team, this can unleash a high level of Chinese support. This has happened with Everton and Manchester City amongst other teams – fuelled by extensive media coverage. Major European competitions can attract hundreds of millions of followers and have helped to make football the most televised sport in China. Support for the national sides however, comes nowhere near this figure. Some top of the table teams attract gates in the tens of thousands, but in the mid-table, teams only tend to attract low gates of 3,000 to 8,000 with 1,000 or less fans for the teams in the relegation zone.

Interestingly, there is also a political backdrop to this sport – the Football Association of China is a government body and not an independent company and the league does not operate independently. This means that the Chinese FA can allow the team to prepare for national competitions by putting a halt to any league games.

Tennis

Like table tennis, a victorious Chinese team allowed the sport to increase in popularity. At the turn of the century, some female Chinese athletes won at the World Championship and a number of victories followed, including a gold medal in the women's tennis double at the 2004 Summer Olympics, the Grand Slam at the Australian Open in 2006 and many others. Tennis has become increasingly popular, and tends to be played at leisure centres and hotels.

Snooker

Ding Junhui is a popular current snooker player. In 2003 he became China's top ranked player and now lives in the UK during the snooker season. In 2005, he defeated British snooker legend Steve Davis in the UK Championship final.

All of his tournaments are widely publicised and scheduled in the Chinese sports calendar.

Grand Prix

The Chinese Grand Prix is a Formula One event held at the Shanghai International Circuit in October every year. The track was designed by the German architect Hermann Tilke and is the most expensive Formula One circuit in the world, costing about $240 million with the capacity for over 200,000 spectators. Around 150,000 tickets were sold for the first race in 2004 and the superb quality of facilities continues to attract a huge audience.

Golf

In China, golf is a symbol of status and a networking tool as well as a sport. It elevates one's status to be a member of a golf club and the sport is widely discussed in business circles. There are around 200 golf courses and clubs in China for amateur golfers, and this number continues to rise year on year. During the last decade, China has developed into one of the most active golfing communities and has attracted several key events to the country – including the PGA European Tour and the Asian PGA Tour in 2004. Volvo, TCL and BMW are all involved in the sponsorship of the sport, indicating its stature in the business world.

Astrology

The Chinese zodiac follows a pattern of 12 years and each year is represented by its own unique creature from the animal kingdom. These take turns as the dominant sign in a particular year – for example, 2007 is the year of the Golden Pig.

亥	Pig	Feb 18 2007 - Feb 06 2008
子	Rat	Feb 07 2008 - Jan 25 2009
丑	Ox	Jan 26 2009 - Feb 13 2010
寅	Tiger	Feb 14 2010 - Feb 02 2011
卯	Rabbit	Feb 03 2011 - Jan 22 2012
辰	Dragon	Jan 23 2012 - Feb 09 2013

巳 Snake	Feb 10 2013 - Jan 30 2014
午 Horse	Jan 31 2014 - Feb 18 2015
未 Sheep	Feb 19 2015 - Feb 07 2016
申 Monkey	Feb 08 2016 - Jan 27 2017
酉 Rooster	Jan 28 2017 - Feb 18 2018
戌 Dog	Feb 19 2018 - Feb 04 2019

Numbers

In the same way that Western cultures are often superstitious with regard to the number 13, the Chinese also attach good and bad omens to numbers.

- "8" is regarded as a lucky number, as the way it is pronounced in the Chinese language sounds similar to the phrase 'to get a fortune'.

- "6" symbolises safety and an easy journey.
- "9" is very lucky – there are nine door knobs positioned horizontally and vertically on the imperial doors in the Forbidden City.
- Doubles are a good omen, for instance a pair of vases, not a single vase, would be given to a newly married couple.
- "73" and "84" are regarded as bad omens for the elderly as they are deemed possible years for death or illness.
- "4" is considered bad luck as its pronunciation is similar to the word for 'death' in Chinese.
- "7" can also be a symbol of death, but this is not as commonly regarded as the number four.

Colours

Colour symbolism is important and it is practical to know what each colour represents in public places:

- Red symbolises good luck and is used for ceremonial purposes. It can be seen at weddings, on slogans and on welcome messages in the New Year.
- In Chinese culture, white is not a symbol of purity but is in fact a symbol of death. This is a very strong perception amongst people who

live in the countryside in particular. However, Western culture has influenced the modern Chinese bride, with white wedding dresses becoming increasingly popular.

- Yellow is reserved exclusively for imperial palaces in China. Although there is no longer a monarchy, the colour is still regarded with reverence.
- The association of pink for girls and blue for boys is not relevant in China.
- Green relates to the Post Office!
- Red represents the ambulance service.
- A hospital is designated by a white background with a red cross.

In Chinese culture there are three central colours: red, black and white.

Red, being the colour of blood, symbolises the positive aspects of life such as happiness, wealth, fame etc. Red is always associated with good luck.

Black, being the colour of faeces is associated with dirt, sin, evil, disasters, sadness, cruelty and suffering amongst other negative things. Black signifies bad fortune and must not be worn during festivals, wedding celebrations or similar happy events. Black should also not be used in home decoration. Whilst black has traditionally symbolised a lack of civilisation and backwardness, traditions associated with this colour are quickly fading, and the younger generation can frequently be seen wearing black as a trendy colour.

White symbolises the mother's milk and is the central ground between red and black, balancing the two colours. It signifies moderation, purity, honesty and life, but is also used at funerals as it is believed that it can harmonise all elements. It can be used in all rituals and ceremonies as it is essentially neutral. Other colours are classified according to their relative darkness and lightness and associated significance with white as the benchmark.

active 英中
anglo chinese communications
创易

Chapter 8

Business Background
Information

Central Chinese Business Structures and Foreign Presence in China

State Owned Enterprises

City-Based State-Owned Enterprises (SOEs) are primarily large businesses operating in key sectors such as the postal industry, communications, transportation, pharmaceuticals, energy and heavy industry. There are reforms in place to stimulate the economy, largely focusing on giving these businesses the freedom to manage their own affairs with complete financial accountability. The state is also reducing its holdings in a number of SOEs by allowing them to convert into companies limited by shares under Company Law and to list their shares on domestic and foreign stock exchanges. The overall number of SOEs has also reduced as a result of mergers and acquisitions.

Collective Enterprises

Collective Enterprises (COEs) are formed by individuals and domestic businesses in rural areas (where approximately 60% of the population resides). The idea of COEs was to foster the rural economy and increase employment opportunities. These are predominantly in the light industrial sector and produce consumer products and can be quite entrepreneurial despite their size. Their volume has shrunk during the period of sustained reform.

Private Enterprises

This term refers to privately owned, often service-orientated businesses. Private Enterprises are becoming an ever more important source of growth and employment in China although they are often located in the coastal provinces, and they remain relatively small.

Companies Limited by Shares

A Company Limited by Shares is very similar to the companies found in other countries and shares can be offered to the public. The minimum amount of registered capital is RMB5 million.

For Company Law to apply to them, SOEs, COEs and private Enterprises must be converted into one of two types of companies: Limited Liability Companies and Companies Limited by Shares. This will help with international investment and globalisation.

Limited Liability Companies

A Limited Liability Company is a legal entity in which the investors' liability is limited to the investment they have made into the company. The company itself is only liable for its obligations based on its total assets, and must have less than 50 shareholders. Capital contributions may be made in cash or in tangible and intangible assets and the minimum capital requirement is RMB30,000.

Representative Offices (ROs)

Due to the expense and complexities involved, international organisations are often wary about setting up a permanent base in China. Initially, it is only permitted by Chinese law for these offices to "build relations and provide technical support" but not to do business directly in China. They can liaise with the relevant Chinese government departments and businesses, undertake market research, gather information and help to sell and source products.

ROs are not permitted to employ local Chinese nationals directly, but must use semi-government sponsored agencies. There is a formal process for this that has simplified significantly as more and more businesses choose this route.

Joint Ventures (JVs)

There are generally two types of Joint Venture formats: Equity Joint Ventures and Co-operative Joint Ventures.

An Equity Joint Venture (EJV) is a limited liability corporation, which is a legal entity in China. The partners in an EJV decide corporate strategy in partnership and each partner owns a proportion of equity share (in equipment, money, rights to the use of a site, factory buildings, industrial pro- perty rights, etc.) They also share the risks, profits and losses according to their share of the equity.

The international partner in an EJV is required by law to take a minimum stake of 25% (there are some exceptions however). Once an EJV expires, it is liquidated but its lifespan can be extended and the international partner is permitted to repatriate their share.

Co-operative Joint Ventures (CJVs) are constructed in a similar legal structure to an EJV but with more flexibility. They are often put in place to manage a short, time-critical project. Under a CJV, the Chinese party provides the JV with the people, property and resources it needs, whilst the international partner brings financial investment, technology or equipment, materials etc. This can help a company ease their way into China whilst managing the level of risk. The links between both parties need to be managed carefully and can be prone to cultural, language and business issues often leading to lengthy delays and potential failure. Making a profit quickly is the best protection against premature failure of the JV and consequent losses. It is important however, to allocate enough resource to make a JV work - it cannot be done in addition to someone's day job.

Wholly Foreign Owned Enterprises (WFOEs)

A Wholly Foreign-Owned Enterprise (WFOE) is a business set up in China from international investment alone, this also includes a JV that is jointly owned by two international investors. This does not apply to just an international office set up in China and it must adhere to Chinese law. Like a JV, the ownership of a WFOE is in the form of equity interests, and there are no shares issued. A lot of them also have definite, albeit extendable, terms of operation. These have been popular due to their flexibility, and because the international investor has more autonomy over the operation without Chinese input. However, the Chinese government can tend to impose tight restrictions on these kinds of organisations i.e. until recently, they were not allowed to sell into the domestic market. Equally, there can be issues associated with the lack of influence from a Chinese business partner - helping to navigate through the many complexities of Chinese industry.

There are a number of advantages of WFOE:

• Autonomy of decision making ithout Chinese

influence;

- Being able to function as a business rather than just an office;
- Being able to invoice in RMB and to pass on these profits to parent companies;
- Protection of intellectual and technological practices;

- Efficiency and control over the destiny of the company;

There is one major disadvantage however: it is dangerous to underestimate the importance of Chinese influence on a business - through cultural know-how, relationship building, localised knowledge and contacts.

Main Issues Facing Businesses in China
Intellectual Property Rights (IPR)
As in the UK, it is key to register any intellectual

property you are keen to preserve with the correct authority. China has signed up to the WTO agreement on Trade-Related Aspects of Intellectual Property Rights (TRIPs Agreement), as well as other intellectual property rights legislation. These apply to licensing imported technology, trade secrets protection and Customs enforcement of IPR. China is also seeking to reform IP law to ensure that it complies with the World Trade Organisation's TRIP'S protocol. There is also a set of laws covering most issues concerning patents, copyrights, trademarks and licensing. The main relevant laws are:

- The Patent Law (1985, amended 1993)
- The Trademark Law (1983, amended 1993)
- The Copyright Law (1991)
- The Unfair Competition Law (1993)

IPR Protection

The main problem IP owners face is poor enforcement of the law. It is broadly accepted that general copyright is the most poorly protected area, while the authorities crack down on people who infringe copyright on registered trademarks fairly effectively. More fundamentally, many government officials in China and the police, have yet to be convinced that infringement of intellectual property can be a serious crime. The Chinese authorities are aware of these problems and they are in the process of being addressed.

From a practical point of view, Customs Officials have the authority to seize shipments of pirated goods. In order to help with the enforcement of this, it maintains a database where foreign companies can record all their Chinese IP registrations.

In the process of doing business with China, it is important to ensure that a thorough investigation of all the options for IPR protection is undertaken. It is safest to appoint an individual in your organisation to ensure that all registrations are completed fully and correctly in accordance with the relevant regulations. IPR registration can be expensive but it is good insurance against problems that may arise later. Proper registration is your strongest weapon against any IPR infringements. To be extra safe, it is recommended to seek the assistance of an experienced lawyer or IPR consultant and in the case of any problems, it is advisable to inform the Embassy, Chamber and relevant Trade Association, as they may be able to help.

Trademarks

Trademarks are registered by the Trademark Office, which is a section of the State Administration of Industry and Commerce. Trademark rights are on a first-to-file basis, not first-to-use and are valid for ten years from the date of registration. Renewal is possible for periods of ten years at a time.

Service companies can register their trade names as 'marks' in the same way that trademarks for goods are registered. However this does not apply to wholesale and retail marks. It is important for international companies or individuals in China that are in the process of applying for registration of a trademark or that have trademark-related issues to appoint a trademark agent designated by the state. Any issues will first be put to the Trademark Review and Adjudication Board, and if they cannot come to a solution, the issue will then go to the People's Court.

Patents

Patents are granted on a first-to-apply basis, which differs from many other countries. Types of patents are:

- Invention: "any new technical solution relating to a product or procedure or relating to an improvement in a product or procedure".
- Utility models: "any new technical solution fit for practical use relating to the shape of a product, its structure, or combinations of the shape or structure of the product". This is easier to attain than the invention patent.
- Designs: "any new design of the shape, colour, pattern, or a combination, creating an aesthetic feeling and suitable for industrial application". This is also relatively easy to achieve.

Patent protection is 20 years for inventions and 10 years for utility models and designs. To pursue a claim against an infringement taking place while the patent is pending, you must serve notice on the person or company that is making the infringement, advising them of your intention. Legal recourse can then be taken once the patent has been granted.

Copyright

Copyright protection in China is comparatively poor, largely because the organisation responsible - the NCAC, seems less capable and less proactive than the other IPR organisations. The legal framework is not the main problem although there are some anomalies with the Berne Convention, and other gaps, which the latest revision of the law is intended to eliminate.

- China's copyright law protects copyrights (including those on works of fine art) for 50 years plus the life of the author, or in employment situations, 50 years from first publication. Works of applied art are protected for 25 years.
- Databases are not protected. It is important to bear in mind, that copyright can belong

to employees rather than employers, and it may therefore be advisable to sign licensing agreements with key employees. Under the law, copyrights can be licensed for ten years although these are renewable.

Licensing

Licensing can be simple i. e. licensing to another party, or licensing by an international investor to the joint venture in which it is investing. The Chinese government strongly encourages technology transfer, and as a result the Chinese side of the agreement may be inclined to see licensed technology as transferred technology. Many foreign investors with valuable IP prefer wholly owned investments to prevent the risk of abuse within a JV.

Due Diligence

The phrase 'due diligence' refers to the careful investigation of a company and its assets, undertaken in order to identify and assess its value and any significant factors that may affect its future performance. Due Diligence studies are essential in measuring the value in an acquisition, merger or joint venture, and in negotiating the terms of a deal. The process must be undertaken by people qualified in the various aspects of the business e.g. technology, legal, financial, environmental, marketing, etc.

It is key to identify the acceptable risks and ensure that the people required to sign off against them are aware of them. It is also important to ascertain what could go wrong, what the hurdles are and who signs off against the deal. It is important to be clear as to who leads the due diligence team and to make sure that they are appraised of their objectives and deadlines. Finally it is vital to be patient, sufficient time must be allowed for due diligence.

Foreign Exchange Controls

As it is still classed as developing country, China continues to impose strict legislative control over international trade. However, to continue its outward facing public policy development and to relieve pressure on RMB revaluation, some relaxation of this control has been allowed. There is now free convertibility permitted on current accounts whilst restricted convertibility is retained on capital accounts. This means that a company with international investment will need to obtain approval from China's foreign

exchange authorities for most kinds of capital account transaction. Those Chinese banks that have been authorised to buy and sell RMB against hard currencies are referred to as designated foreign exchange banks (DFXBs).

The Chinese Perception of Law and Contracts in Business

The Chinese court system still suffers from a poor reputation. In the 1980's when China's economy began, the courts were widely perceived as a forum for either sentencing criminals or getting divorced, and a Judge as just another type of government official. However, people are using the court system more and more and China is currently facing an explosion of legal proceedings. Figures are showing that China boasts in excess of 4,000 courts which are now struggling to cope with the strain of handling five million cases a year, up from only a few hundred thousand, two decades ago.

The courts have improved significantly in recent years and it appears that people now have increased confidence in the court system, demonstrated by the growth in trials and lawsuits.

The Financial Times reported that the opinion among foreign lawyers is that proceedings have become "markedly more professional" and that "lawsuits are often decided on their legal merits".

Despite this, the Chinese under-standing of a contract is quite different from a Westerner's point of view. Contracts themselves are in fact, a fairly new concept for the majority of Chinese companies. Chinese businesspeople can find the many "seemingly unnecessary" legal clauses confusing and the specially phrased legal contents incomprehensible, even for English-speaking Chinese people. The language is one of the biggest issues when discussing a contract. Contracts are generally written in English with a Chinese version as a reference, and to translate a contract from one language to another is no simple task. Because of the legality and the indefinite nature of language, the translated version doesn't always work for the other party. Sometimes poor translation can be the cause, but more often it is the unfamiliarity of the legal terms and the level of formality from the Chinese side. However, it is recommended to be cautious before having a lawyer present in a business meeting. China is more of a moral society than a legal one. In China, whenever unexpected circumstances arise, they are typically sorted out through the strong relationship bonds that exist. In the face of a lawyer, the Chinese can adopt a highly guarded attitude and the situation can be soured from the start. It is definitely advisable to bring your technical experts to the negotiation table. As in any negotiation you need to be sure that relationship issues are also considered as part of the terms of the negotiation.

Chinese businesspeople and Westerners often approach negotiations from opposite poles: since commercial law is part of our everyday lives, the Western approach is to start with a contract, altering it as necessary and signing the final revised version. Traditionally, commercial law has scarcely existed in China and would indicate lack of faith in the partner with whom the contract is to be signed. Accordingly even today a signed contract is merely regarded as a symbol of progress, with the completed contract only demonstrating that both sides have grown close enough to develop a trusting relationship.

Business Negotiation

Be prepared, a negotiation in China can be a long, drawn out process. As the Chinese businessperson prefers to do business with people they know and are friendly with, the process is treated as part of the development of a solid relationship. As a result, flying visits are regarded as disrespectful, as they indicate that your Chinese counterparts are of low priority to your organisation. The Chinese generally expect their Western visitors' trip to last for a few days. During the time you spend on your business trip, they will make well considered plans to not only demonstrate their business strength, but to also demonstrate China's great cultural assets including at least a visit to the Great Wall and to see the Terracotta Soldiers. The Chinese hospitality is renowned.

Proceedings often commence with a discussion in which the importance of a mutually beneficial and long-term relationship is emphasised. Eagerness to sign a contract without paving a harmonious path will not be well regarded.

It depends on the Chinese organisation you are dealing with, but inevitably some government officials are involved at some stage. Because of the political background and structure in China, a representative of the government or the state will need to be involved. They are keen to be seen to support local businesses and in addition, no company can succeed without their local government department's help. Under the general economic climate in China, government officials are also under pressure to meet their targets, and as such, have another reason to get involved.

A negotiation normally includes two distinct phases - the technical and the commercial phase. With a bigger Chinese organisation, several teams may come together to form a central negotiating team. The technical phase can be very detailed and you would need to send someone representative and competent not just technically, but also good at simplifying complicated issues, without going into too much detail. The number of your negotiation team members is also worth considering. Facing more than twenty members of your partner organisation's team, one or two of your own team may be far too out-numbered, in addition, it could also be regarded as an indication that this particular project is of low priority for your organisation.

Because of the hierarchical management structure in China, a decision has to be made either collectively or from the top filtered down.

Likewise be prepared to involve representatives of local, regional or even national government in your negotiations. These people may not have any shares in the company, but the success of the company may strengthen their own position or give them valuable experience in order to further their own career.

Written contracts are not as important as personal commitments between associates. However, it is important to bear in mind the fact that Chinese people would sometimes rather say what they think you would like to hear, than tell you the truth. They therefore do not like to say 'no' in a business meeting or admit that they do not understand something. Be aware that "maybe" or "I'll think about it" usually means "no". To get the bottom of a situation, other research channels such as talking via the interpreter or your direct contact behind the scenes may prove to be effective.

Western business visitors are often deadline-driven, but this is not necessarily so in China and can be a cause of frustration. Businesspeople with experience in these negotiations know how long internal consultations on the Chinese side can take. However, Chinese negotiators can move extremely fast on other occasions and will sometimes use this change of pace to put pressure on their prospective partners to agree to their plan of action.

Whilst the Western approach to negotiations is based on logic, the Chinese approach will probably be influenced by early philosophers who recognise a paradoxical balance of opposites in all things. Where Westerners tend to look for clear alternatives, the Chinese in general may examine ways to combine both options. This difference in approach may give the impression that a Chinese negotiator is being illogical, evasive or devious, when they believe they are being quite straightforward. It is important to make an allowance for this kind of difference of approach in any negotiation process.

Think about the dynamics of your meetings carefully. A Chinese colleague will often be effective in assisting by advising at meetings, which member of the negotiating team holds the most sway – this is not always obvious. Also, think about who you take with you - Chinese partners will often see a visit by a Western company's representatives and their seniority in their corporate hierarchy as an indication of sincerity and commitment. A Chinese lawyer may be necessary for advice on Chinese law, but as previously mentioned, taking a lawyer should be considered with care as it could be regarded as a sign of distrust.

Researching the Market

Some companies are lucky enough to find a suitable Chinese partner with relative ease, either through its own network of contacts or existing customers, or through internet enquiries. However, for the majority it involves many trial-and-error attempts, a significant investment of time and a few intensive visits to China.

It is essential to carry out some market research prior to visiting. With the advent of the internet, collating information has been made very easy. However, finding a reliable and current source can be a challenge, so cross-referencing is important. There are also a variety of international and Chinese research companies available, the international research companies tend to charge more but are better equipped to cater for a Western company's requirements. On

the other hand, Chinese research companies may charge less and may also have better information channels.

Having researched the market on paper and checked out this information with anyone you know who has worked with China, it is essential to visit the market yourself. This will give you a personal understanding of the scale and feel of the country, you will also soak up the vibrant entrepreneurial atmosphere. A good starting point would be a well targeted trade fair where you will be able to talk to many potential direct suppliers, customers and partners all under one roof. Meantime, you can also investigate the Chinese market as a whole in terms of product variety and quality. At the same time, if you could manage to visit a few relevant companies or factories, it would make your trip even more worthwhile.

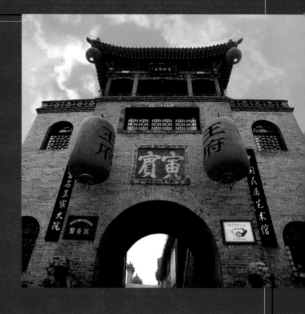

active 英中
创易
anglo chinese communications

Chapter 9

Business Travel
Information

Visa Applications

Visas are required by overseas visitors entering mainland China, but not for Western nationals visiting Hong Kong and Macau. Visas are available from Chinese embassies and consulates in most countries. Applying for a visa from the

Chinese Embassy is not a complicated procedure but queuing times can be unpredictable. An alternative option would be to consider contacting a visa agency, which obtains tourist or business visas for its clients without them having

to queue up at an embassy, subject to payment of an additional processing fee.

Single, double and multiple entry visas are available, although it is advisable to check with the Embassy beforehand regarding the information that needs to accompany the application.

A useful tip is that if a visa has been issued to you on a previous visit, then you may wish to consider an overnight stay in Hong Kong where hotel-based travel agents offer a same day or next day visa service. Multi-entry visas can usually be obtained by this method as well. Most nationalities need only a valid passport to enter Hong Kong.

For more detailed information please see www. chinese-embassy.org.uk/eng/. You can download the application form beforehand. Please note the opening hours and holidays of the embassy.

Health Requirements

- No vaccinations are currently required for China, except for yellow fever if you are arriving from an area where the disease is endemic. However, you should discuss your trip with your doctor who will have updated information regarding any potential health issues.

- Precautions against malaria, typhoid and cholera are recommended for travellers planning to visit certain rural areas (mainly Hainan Island in the Yunnan province and Guangxi province).
- Travel insurance is advised for trips to China. If you're not already covered you should contact a specialist travel insurance company.
- Prior to departing, it would be wise to check the following websites for essential travel advice:

  www.masta-travel-health.com or

  www.fitfortravel.nhs.uk

You can discuss any particular needs you may have with your own doctor or nurse prior to the commencement of your visit to China.

Flights to China

China's most important long-haul international gateways are Beijing, Hong Kong, Guangzhou and Shanghai, although many other Chinese cities are served by international flights, operated mainly by airlines based in East Asia. Tickets for direct flights to China are easily available, except during peak seasons (for example, February during Chinese New Year, or summer holiday season for students) when you are advised to book as far in advance as possible.

Single and group tickets are available and most tickets can be purchased over the phone, internet, directly from airline companies or from travel agents. Most airline companies now use e-tickets (except Chinese airlines), and will send a confirmation of your flight details to your e-mail address. The direct airlines include Air China, British Airways, China Eastern Airlines, Virgin Atlantic Airways, Cathy Pacific Airways, Air

New Zealand, Qantas Airways and the recently launched low cost 'no-frills' airline Oasis Hong Kong. However, if you can bear a longer journey and prefer to get a bargain - indirect flights from other European or even Mid-Eastern cities are well worth looking into.

Accommodation

The quality of hotels in China varies enormously, both in terms of comfort and service. As in most developed countries, you can expect to find accommodation to suit every pocket, from 'six star' executive hotels down to very basic rooms which are barely suitable for tourist needs. Generally, there are a large number of premium and international chain hotels in big cities. They offer excellent services and have a wide range of amenities such as air conditioning, satellite TV and often a mini-bar and broadband internet connection. However, hotels in small or remote towns usually only have basic amenities. If business facilities are essential to your visit, it is better to stay in international or chain hotels, as they are likely to be more familiar with international business visitors' needs. If you plan to enjoy some leisure time on your trip, local hotels may be more suitable as they are often more historical, with a strong sense of local culture, or occupy the best and most scenic locations. Visit www.bb-china.com for accommodation which incorporates the personality of the region.

During the peak seasons, it is advisable to book rooms in advance and confirm your reservations, as they are usually very busy or fully booked. It's also worth considering that in popular tourist destinations during the peak season, hotels can charge considerably more.

When travelling around the city, it is advisable to carry a card with your hotel's name and address written on it in Chinese, so that if you get lost,

you can hand the card to a local resident in order to help you back to your hotel! Contact cards are available at service desks or receptions in most hotels. Hotel staff will be happy to write down where you want to go and often make a note of the taxi registration number and hand it to you. This is useful if you leave anything in the taxi or have a reason to complain.

Other practical points:
- Accounts in large hotels can be paid with credit cards though it is advisable to have either traveller's cheques or some exchangeable currency for situations where cash is required.
- Often you will find that there are cups and kettle for making tea/coffee in each room.
- Water is easily available in China, but never drink tap water. Bottled or boiled water is always on hand in hotels and you can buy bottled spring water at stalls and shops.

Travel Insurance
Although not essential, it is strongly advisable that you are covered by travel insurance, in case of theft, loss or medical problems. Most travel agents are able to provide you with insurance.

For more detailed information, visit www.travel-insurance.net/info

Illness

Medical advice and care are provided by hospitals as there are no GP equivalents in China. Should you need it, the hotel staff, your local contact or hotel representative will call you a doctor or more likely, arrange for you to be taken to a hospital. Larger hospitals in major cities usually have departments dedicated to foreign patients with staff that speak good English.

For minor complaints, every town has a pharmacy that can suggest remedies, and doctors who can treat you with traditional Chinese or Western techniques. Chinese herbal medicine is usually used in conjunction with Western medicine. However, you may request to use solely Western drugs. Pharmacies offer a large range of non-prescription and some prescription drugs. Outside of major conurbations, it is advisable to either take along your translator.

Arrival

Passengers arriving from abroad have to complete

health certificates when passing through the Quarantine Check area. The Border Control Area is then passed through, where you need to show your passport to the official along with your Entry Registration Card (these will be distributed on the plane en route to China). Customs forms are cleared as usual on exit from the baggage claim area. Cash machines and banks are available at airports. There may be people at the airport touting for taxi business, in which case, it is better to find a proper taxi station to avoid being tricked.

Time Zone

The time in China is set to Beijing time, which is GMT +8 hours in winter time and GMT +7 hours in summer time.

Electricity

The voltage in China is 220 volts. Socket types are typically two round or flat pins, or three angled prolonged pins. Adaptors can usually be borrowed from the hotel.

Business Hours

China officially has a five day working week but there may be regional or industry variances. The Chinese people tend to follow the same rigid meal routine: 12 noon for lunch, 6pm for dinner. Opening hours for other facilities can differ significantly. Here is a basic guide to some of them, however, be mindful that this is for reference only. It is better to check with locals to be absolutely sure.

Government Offices: 8.30am – 5/6pm, with an hour's midday lunch break in the winter and two hours in the summer.

Shops: Department stores are usually open from 9am to 7pm (8pm or even 10pm in summer) seven days a week.

Banks: In hotels, banks tend to be open from

7.30am or 8am to around 7pm, seven days a week, with a break for lunch. (In larger hotels, foreign exchange facilities stay open later). Banks outside hotels are usually open from 9am to 5.30pm, and may have a one hour lunch break. Most banks are open on Saturdays and Sundays.

Post Offices: Branches in hotels operate from 8am to 6pm, Monday to Saturday, and Sunday mornings from 8am to noon. Post Offices outside hotels are usually open from 9am to 5pm, and are open on Saturdays and Sundays.

Restaurants: Opening hours for large restaurants are usually 10am to 11pm. Smaller restaurants

have very flexible opening hours, open early in the morning and close late at night. However, should you wish to dine at a more Mediterranean time, you may find yourself accompanied by nothing more than the restaurant cat.

Museums: Opening hours are usually 9am to 5pm; they stay open at weekends but close on Monday or another day mid-week.

Spas and Salons

All large hotels have a salon and spa and during a tiring business trip, you could take the time out to relax and enjoy the facilities on offer. Facial, body and foot massages are available upon request in your room or at the spa. Most hotels are well equipped with a gym, swimming pool, jacuzzi, sauna and often a steam room.

Going to a spa or a massage parlour for a relaxing session is a favourite local pastime for the Chinesse people. You will easily find a place outside of your hotel that offers a more extensive range of treatments at a much cheaper rate. The hotel staff are mormally happy to recommend somewhere suitable.

Currency

Renminbi (RMB) means 'the people's currency'. Its basic unit is 'Yuan' or in speech 'Kuai'. The Yuan is also divided into 10 'jiao' (or 'mao'), again divided into 'fen', but these units are of such a low value that they are becoming less commonly used.

Currency Exchange: foreign currency and traveller's cheques can be exchanged for RMB very easily in hotels with your passport as proof of identity. Banks also have this function but this facility is usually only found in the larger cities. You should keep your receipt safe, in case you want to convert excess Chinese money back into foreign currency when leaving the country.

Credit Cards: Major international credit cards such as Visa, MasterCard and American Express are widely accepted at hotels, large department stores and major restaurants and bars. For smaller cities and towns, local credit/cash cards or cash are far more convenient.

ATM Machines: ATMs are widely accessible and can be used to withdraw money in major cities, airports or shopping centres. Almost all banks have a 24 hour ATM attached to the branch, so to be able to identify the banks' logos would prove to be useful during your visit. The Bank of China controls the main foreign-friendly ATMs.

Bank of China ATMs operate both in Chinese and English (depending on your card), use the latest equipment, and are pretty easy to find.

Whilst it is easy to access, it doesn't always mean that the machine has sufficient money inside, especially during the festival seasons, holidays or weekends. The most common withdrawal limit is 5000 Yuan or 6000 Yuan but some machines set a 2000 lower Yuan limit than the others. It doesn't stop you from taking out a withdrawal several times however! You can press the 'continue' button and try to get more cash out up to the ATM's daily limit.

Transport

Domestic Flights

There are several domestic airlines providing a good level of service using modern planes, and covering the whole of the country. Moving between regions therefore is fast and easy. There are frequent flights throughout the day between major cities. Flying is a luxury worth considering for long distances: prices are similar to soft-sleeper train travel but journey times are far less. The planes are generally relatively new and well maintained and the service is good – soft drinks, biscuits and souvenir trinkets are handed out along the way, and sometimes there's even a raffle!

It is crucial to plan ahead when booking internal air travel in China, especially during the Chinese New Year and the public holidays. Tickets can easily be arranged through the travel agencies found in all major hotels.

Airports

There are 11 international airports in China – Beijing, Shanghai, Guangzhou (Canton), Tianjin, Urumqi, Hangzhou, Kunming, Shenyang, Dalian,

Harbin and Xiamen.

The Beijing Capital International Airport is the most popular arrival point for foreign visitors and is in the midst of a major capital investment programme in anticipation of the arrival of the

Olympics Games in Beijing in the summer of 2008. There is a wide range of facilities at major airports, especially at Beijing and Shanghai.

ATM machines, banks, cafés, snack bars and duty-free shops can be found easily. Restaurants serve a wide range of food, including Chinese food, fast-food and many other types.

Trains
China's rail network is vast, efficient and the

safest, most reliable way to get around the country.

The express train from Shanghai to Beijing is one of the key business train links in the rail network. You could save time and money by travelling overnight; however, you should consider whether sharing an enclosed area of space with

complete strangers is really for you! In addition, the facilities and services provided on the rail network are not as efficient as airports, so you should give consideration to this point if you are travelling with large amounts of luggage.

There is also a new generation of bullet trains that can travel up to a speed of 250kph; and these have been welcomed by China's main cities. Although they are more expensive than normal trains, bullet trains can cut up to two hours off the average journey time between major cities compared to traditional trains.

Most major cities are linked to Beijing, whilst Shanghai and Tianjin offer regional and national links too. A total of 60 bullet trains leave Beijing every day and offer very comfortable and spacious seats and a full range of services and amenities.

One of China's key transportation developments was the introduction in 2004 of the world's first commercial magnetic levitation line. The Maglev (magnetic levitation) trains link Shanghai city centre and Pudong International Airport. Travelling at 500mph, you will be able to experience travelling at the speed of a jet aircraft on the ground, with the 30 kilometre trip taking only eight minutes.

Taxis

Taxis in China are cheap and plentiful, and, as a rule they tend to be the most convenient way to get around Chinese cities. Rates vary depending on which city you are travelling in, with Beijing, Shenzhen, and Shanghai being the most expensive places to catch a cab. Taxis range from one Yuan to two Yuan per kilometre, with passengers usually expected to pay for any toll charges. In smaller cities this may not be the case. It is wise to check with the hotel before your trip so that you know the rough price.

It is important to retain all your receipts in case you need to recover any lost goods or make a complaint if you have an issue with the fare you have been asked to pay. If you have to go outside of the city or you are planning to make lots of different visits in a day, it may be worth hiring a taxi (or a chauffeured car) for the day. It is more expensive to book through the hotel but your local contact can often get you a good price or simply find a taxi driver that is friendly and negotiate a good deal. It may not be the cheapest option but if you need to meet lots of people within a tight schedule, you will find it is well worth it. It is important to have your destination written down in Chinese characters before taking a cab.

Roads and Driving

In mainland China the traffic drives on the right-hand side of the road. Hong Kong and Macao drive on the left. You can drive with an International Driver's License for a limited amount of time (a minimum of half a year), after which a Chinese licence is required. Having experienced the increasingly worsening traffic, parking slots and the different style of the local driving, it may be wise not to drive yourself on your first visit to China!

Metro

The subway is very cheap e.g. three Yuan per single ticket in Beijing, for example. It offers a fast and frequent method of travelling but can be extremely crowded during rush hour. Off peak, it can be a perfect way to cut through the dense traffic.

Tipping and Bartering

Tipping is not customary in China, but visitors should be aware that local attitudes on tipping are changing, and vary with the occasion. It is the norm to tip hotel staff such as the porters and the concierge. Some tourists bring along inexpensive gifts to show their appreciation to guides, drivers or other people who have been helpful.

Bargaining is acceptable in most markets, but not in the supermarket or some shopping centres. Informal markets are the best places to bargain, as the goods are quoted at 200% to 300% of the actual price. Half of the price is achievable, a third would prove your negotiation skills, and you would deserve a medal if you get your shirt at a quarter of the original price! These markets are well worth a visit for a businessperson as it may prove to be an effective training ground to polish your negotiation skills.

Eating and Drinking

The Chinese love to eat, and from market-stall buns and soup right through to the intricate variations of regional cookery, China boasts one of the world's greatest cuisines.

Eating and dining are a very important part of Chinese culture. Meals are considered to be major social events, and the process is geared accordingly to a group of diners sharing a variety of different dishes with their companions. You are sure to find some favourites, whether it be rice, noodles, meat, seafood, vegetables or a mixture of all of these.

Increasingly, more restaurants are offering food from other countries such as Japanese, Indian, Thai and Western cuisine. Cafés and fast food restaurants are also becoming more popular so there is even more to choose from! Most restaurants and cafés are very hygienic. Smaller

restaurants in smaller cities may not be as hygienic, so it may not be a bad idea to be more cautious if you find yourself in a restaurant of this kind.

More restaurants now provide you with a knife and fork. However, most are still not equipped with these so your ability to use chopsticks is sure to have improved by the end of your trip! It is advisable not to eat raw food, unless of course you are eating Sushi. Tap water in China is not drinkable; always drink bottled, boiled or filtered water.

Communication Facilities

Mobile Phones

Tri-band mobiles work throughout all the regions of China that business travellers are likely to visit. Major British networks offer roaming services in China so it should not be difficult to stay in touch. You can make and receive calls and texts to the UK but for convenience, you may choose to purchase a Chinese SIM card to make local calls. Chinese SIM cards work in most British mobiles. There is a charge for both making and receiving calls. The major networks in China are ChinaMobile and ChinaUnicom.

Laptops

Whilst wireless connections are not widespread, their availability is growing quickly. Wireless availability in four and five star hotels is increasing.

Mail

You can easily access your email account if you have an internet connection, although certain Western websites may prove to take longer to access. In particular, in response to the perceived threat of free access to information, the government has reportedly constructed a firewall to block access to politically sensitive sites.

Internet Cafés

Domestic interest in the internet is huge, and with personal computer ownership still low,

there are internet café facilities throughout the country offering a fairly fast broadband internet connection at very reasonable rates. However, most cafés do not permit memory stick access and printing facilities are not widely available. The business centres that you will find in most big hotels offer fax, telephone, internet and other services such as photocopying and secretarial assistance.

Blackberry Access
These can be used via the ChinaMobile network. However, some functions may not be available such as videocall.

Telephones

Nearly all hotel rooms are equipped with a telephone. Some are free of charge when dialling local calls but do check with the hotel. There will be a charge for international or domestic calls, including intra and inter-provincial calls. Alternatively, payphones in phone booths or newspaper stands are readily available. Local and international phone cards can be purchased easily.

Travel Hazards

Official statistics show a comparatively low

incidence of crimes against foreign visitors. Normal precautions apply; in general you can walk around safely, day or night. Beware of pickpockets in crowded areas such as in sightseeing destinations, airports, markets and department stores. With extremely busy traffic in most major cities, be careful when crossing the road. Vehicles rarely stop for pedestrians at zebra crossings unless at traffic lights so look carefully in both directions before you cross.

Local English Assistance

The most widely-read English language newspapers are the China Daily and People's Daily, available at hotels in most major cities, as well as some smaller cities. Other papers such as the China News Digest, Eastday, South China Morning Post, Inside China Today and regional papers, for example, the Shanghai Daily and Shanghai Star are also available in English. The most popular English language magazines include China Today and China Pictorial. Some business-related magazines include City Weekend, China Briefing and magazines with regional information such as Beijing Review and That's Shanghai.

Top Ten Most Popular Souvenirs:

- Olympic souvenirs
- Jade carvings
- Silk products such as silk scarves
  and table cloths
- Jade and pearl jewellery
- Chinese brush paintings on rice paper
- Chopping stamps of various materials,
  engraved with your name or a message
- Miniature terracotta soldiers
- Chinese tea and tea sets
- Chinese cookery books
- Lacquer handicrafts

Chapter 10

Arranging
Your Visiting Time

National Holidays

There are 11 national public holidays in the Chinese calendar:

- New Year's Day (January 1st): 1 day
- Chinese New Year or 'Spring Festival' (usually falling in late January or early and mid-February): 3 days
- Labour Day (May 1st): 1 day
- Tomb Sweeping Day (5th April): 1 day
- Dragon Boat Festival (the 5th day of the 5th Lunar month, usually in June): 1 day
- Mid Autumn Day (the 15th day of the 8th Lunar month, usually in September/October): 1 day
- National Day (October 1st): 3 days

Offices and agencies in China generally work a 5-day week. The weekend days adjacent to a national holiday are usually moved to form a longer holiday period so that people will have three days or seven days off in a row

The following days are holidays for particular groups of people:

- March 8th: International Women's Day (a half day holiday for women)

- May 4th: Youth Day (a half day holiday for people aged 14 - 20)
- June 1st: Children's Day (a full day holiday for all children aged 13 and under)
- July 1st: Birthday of the Communist Party
- August 1st: Army Day (for armed forces personnel)
- September 1st: Teacher's Day

Traditional Chinese Events and Celebrations

Chinese New Year (also called 'Spring Festival') is the most important of all Chinese traditions. It starts on the first day of the lunar calendar, usually in February and is very similar in a lot of ways to the Christmas celebrated in the West.

Officially it is only a 3 day holiday but it often lasts for a week or an even longer period. It is a family celebration and to be united with the family during this holiday is essential. Big cities that are normally full of people from other provinces or rural areas become ghost towns over this time. People stay indoors, taking part in many traditional family rituals such as making dumplings, playing 'mahjongg', putting up posters to stop evil spirits from coming in and even cleaning the house to prepare for the year ahead.

The Lantern Festival is celebrated on the 15th day after Chinese New Year. It is not a public holiday, but it marks the end of the New Year celebrations and provides another opportunity for a family reunion, called small New Year or "Yuan Xiao Festival" as people eat a particular kind of sweet dumpling during this holiday. The famous Lion Dances are also traditionally enjoyed during this festival.

Tomb Sweeping Day is the 5th April. Many Chinese people observe the day with traditional tomb-cleaning activities. It is an opportunity to pay tribute to the dead in various rituals and marks of respect.

The Dragon Boat Festival takes place on the 5th day of the 5th lunar month, usually in June. People eat Zongzi (rice wraps) and drink yellow rice wine to commemorate the greatest patriotic poet in Chinese history - Qu Yuan. During this time, Hong Kong hosts one of the liveliest annual Chinese celebrations.

The Chinese Valentine's Day or Magpie Festival (Qi Xi) is celebrated by lovers and couples alike on the 7th day of the 7th lunar month. It originates from a well-known Chinese tale where two lovers, Niulang and Zhinu, would only meet once a year on this day on a bridge in the heavens.

Mid-Autumn Festival is celebrated on the 15th day of the 8th lunar month, sometime in September or October. It is a chance for farmers to celebrate a good harvest and for families to meet, admire the full moon and eat moon-cake together.

The Double Ninth Festival (Chong Yang Festival) follows a tradition of mountain climbing, admiring Chinese chrysanthemums, eating cake and drinking Chinese wine. It falls on the 9th day of the 9th lunar month (usually in October).

The Laba Festival which is celebrated on the 8th day of the 12th lunar month (normally in January) is traditionally, an opportunity for people to pray to the Gods for a good harvest and good fortune. Now, families gather and eat Laba porridge together, which contains a variety of ingredients such as dates, lily flower seeds and nuts.

Major Forthcoming International Events

- 8th – 24th August, 2008: The Olympic Games
- 1st May – 31st October, 2010: World Expo 2010 Shanghai

Mix Business with Pleasure – China's Top Ten 'Must See' Attractions

China is a vast country, and as such has a great

many attractions for international visitors. These are the top ten 'must see' attractions according to feedback from Western travellers:

Great Wall, Beijing

The Great Wall has a history dating back over 2000 years. The first part of the Wall was built under the orders of the first Emperor of China - Qing Shi Huang - between 220 and 200 BC and was fortified during the Ming Dynasty in the 16th century. In ancient times, it was used as a form of defence against invading armies. Now, it is a Chinese cultural landmark, a UNESCO World Heritage Site and one of the Seven Wonders of the World. The Wall stretches for approximately 6,400km, from the Jiayu Pass in the West to the Shanhai Pass in the East. The most famous sections of the Wall are Badaling and Mutianyu, the former of which is well-known for its breath-taking geological features and whilst it is the most perfectly preserved part of the Wall, it is also the most congested. The Mutianyu section is a little further away but much quieter and less busy with tourists. Other lesser-known sections such as Gubeikou, Jinshanling and Simatai are not as well restored, but are more authentic and offer a more relaxed opportunity for visitors to view this national treasure.

Terracotta Army, Xian

The Terracotta Army was buried with the first Emperor of China around 210BC. Its role was to help to rule the empire of Qin Shi Huang in the after-life. The site was discovered in 1974 by local farmers who were drilling water holes. Each of the warrior figures has

unique features and accessories and is made life-sized and extremely realistic. Many stone horse carriages, crafted weapons, tools and treasures were also buried alongside them.

The Forbidden City, Beijing

First built in 1406, 24 Emperors of the Ming and Qing Dynasties lived and reigned here. It has more than 9,000 rooms and spans a large area of 720,000m². It is also known as the Palace Museum and has the world's largest collection of preserved ancient wooden structures. It exemplifies the essence of Chinese imperial architecture, which has influenced the architectural development and culture of other countries in East Asia.

Summer Palace, Beijing

This is the largest and most well-preserved royal garden in China. It was first built in 1750 and

was then rebuilt in 1888 for the Empress Dowager CiXi of the Qing Dynasty. It occupies around 2.9million m² and has beautiful surroundings with many temples and halls – all of which are well worth a visit. United Nations Educational, Scientific and Cultural Organization (UNESCO) declared the Summer Palace an "outstanding expression of the creative art of Chinese landscape garden design, incorporating the works of humankind and nature in a harmonious whole".

Temple of Heaven, Beijing

Constructed in 1420, the Emperors of the Ming

and Qing Dynasties used this site for worshipping heaven and praying for a good harvest. Now, it is the largest and most well-preserved complex of imperial altars in China. It is four times the size of the Forbidden City and with much greenery, magnificent temples and a pleasant environment throughout the year, the place is well worth a visit.

The Bund, Shanghai

The Bund is the most famous tourist attraction in Shanghai and stretches for a mile along the Western bank of the Huangpu River. 52 buildings, constructed in a wide range of architectural styles are situated along the Bund, representing the Gothic, Baroque, Romanesque, Renaissance, Neo-Classical and Art Deco styles. The buildings house some of the most famous

banks and hotels in China. The view at night is especially beautiful and its grandeur can be appreciated by standing on the other side of the river bank or taking a cruise along the river.

Guilin, Guangxi province

Guilin is one of the oldest cities in the Guangxi province. It is an extremely popular and famous tourist destination both for its culture and unique natural environment. It has strange mountains in which shapes of animals and characters in Chinese novels and myths can be made out. The Li Jiang River has beautiful scenery along

its banks such as mountains and rocks, a view which can be enjoyed whilst taking a trip down the river.

Jiu Zhai Gou, Sichuan province

Located in the Sichuan Province, its name originates from the 9 Tibetan villages in its gully. The gully has a total length of more than 80km and is famous for its beautiful springs, lakes, waterfalls, snow mountains and forests. Its quiet, natural and undisturbed environment will be an excellent escape from the hectic pace of life in the city!

Suzhou Traditional Garden, the Jiangsu province

There are several traditional Gardens in Suzhou,

part of the Jiangsu province. Most were constructed in the Ming Dynasty and the most famous is the Zhuozheng Garden. Each has its own unique features with calm lakes and rooms where the Emperor and his family used to live during their visits.

Harbin Ice Lantern Festival, Heilongjiang province

Harbin is the capital of the Heilongjiang province, the most Northern province of China. The temperature can hit depths as low as -30°C, hence it is ideally positioned for its spectacular exhibitions of ice sculptures based on animals, plants, buildings or motifs taken from legends. The festival is normally held in January and February each year but it can unofficially start from December and go on until early March.

Test Your Knowledge of China

- What is the main spoken language used in China?
- What is the current population of China?
- What are the 'four major inventions' most talked about by the Chinese people?
- When was the People's Republic of China established?
- How many municipal cities are there in China?
- Who is the most influential philosopher in the Chinese history?
- What metric system does China use - imperial or metric?
- What does RMB stand for and what does it mean?
- What were the first Emperor - Qinshihuang's - major achievements in history (name three)?
- Name the two Special Administrative Regions in China.
- Which major event is going to take place in Shanghai in 2010?
- Name three of the Chinese government's current major concerns.
- What's the meaning of Guanxi?
- What does 'face' represent?

Metric and Chinese Measurement Conversions

Temperature

$°C = (°F - 32) ÷ 1.8$
$°F = (°C × 1.8) + 32$
$28°C ≈ 82°F$

Weight

'jin' (斤) and 'liang' (两) are the traditional Chinese units for weight measurement
1jin = 10 liang
1lb = 0.45kg = 0.91 jin
1kg = 2.2lb = 2 jin
1oz = 28g
1g = 0.04oz

Volume

1L = 0.22 imperial gallons = 0.26 US gallon
1 imperial gallon = 1.2 US gallons = 4.55L
1 US gallon = 0.83 imperial gallons = 3.8L

Length

'zhang' (丈) , 'chi' (尺) , 'cun' (寸) are traditional Chinese units of distance measurement which are still in use at times
1 zhang = 10 chi
1 chi = 10 cun
1 m = 3 chi
1 in = 2.54 cm = 0.076 chi
1 cm = 0.39 in = 0.03 chi
1ft = 0.3 m = 0.91 chi
1 m = 3.3 ft = 1.1 yd = 3 chi
1 mile = 1.6 km
1 km = 0.62 miles

Area

'mu' (亩) is the traditional Chinese unit of area measurement which is still in use at times:
1 mu = 0.07 hectare = 0.17 acres (837 sq yards)
1 hectare = 2.47 acres = 15 mu
1 acre = 0.40 hectares = 6.07 mu

Travel Tips: Don't Leave Home Without Them!

Planning your trip:

- Check the dates of major national holidays and events when arranging a visit to China. Avoid these periods if you can.
- Bring all the essentials you may need with you – from personal items, medicines, through to stationery, as it is wise to never assume you can get it easily in China.
- Make sure you have a sufficient supply of adaptors - otherwise, check with your hotel in advance.
- Be prepared with plenty of business cards (in Chinese).
- Take some small souvenirs with you as 'gift giving' is a way of life in China.
- When making an appointment for a meeting, be mindful of potential traffic delays and factor in some extra time.

Staying in a hotel:

- Western chain hotels are generally better equipped to accommodate Westerners' business needs.

- Try to stay in hotels that are near your meeting locations to avoid traffic delays.
- In an emergency, the business centre staff may offer flexible office hours – it is always worth checking if this facility will be available.
- The concierge is the best person in the hotel to ask for local information.
- Always carry your hotel card with its address and telephone details on it.
- It is not recommended to drink tap water - you should always drink boiled water or mineral water to be safe. Be careful when using ice.

Practical matters:

- When writing the date in China, the order is: Year – Month – Day.
- When writing an address in China, the order is: country – province – city – district – street number – the person's name.
- The 'ground floor' is the first floor in China.
- An internet café is not suitable for business use, they don't normally have a printer and the use of a memory stick is often barred.
- A local mobile sim card is a great money saver for frequent visitors.
- The Chinese dine at 12 noon for lunch and at

6pm for dinner.

- Always keep taxi receipts so that you can trace any lost goods or make a complaint.
- If your taxi has no meters, always negotiate the price before getting in.
- Many train services may seem straightforward but be mindful that they do not offer the same level of service as the airport.
- Always have a comfortable pair of shoes with you – China is a large country!
- There is zero tolerance for drinking and driving in China.
- It's always wise to carry some toilet paper with you and be prepared to squat as the toilets are not the same as you would find in the West!
- Always carry sufficient cash - credit cards are not generally accepted at local shops or restaurants.
- A limited amount of cash can be drawn out of an ATM machine from one account at one time. You can repeat this process if you require more transactions.
- You need a passport to exchange cash at a hotel or bank. Be aware that the locals are more sensitive about torn notes, so undamaged ones will be easier to use.